TRUE BLUE

TRIUMPH
BOOKS

Published by Triumph Books, Chicago.

Text by John Oehser.

Photography by AJ Macht, Don Larson and Jason Chapman unless indicated otherwise

Content packaged by Mojo Media, Inc.
Editor: Joe Funk
Creative Director: Jason Hinman

This book is available in quantity at special discounts for your group or organization.
For further information, contact:

Triumph Books
542 South Dearborn Street
Suite 750
Chicago, IL 60605

Chicago, Illinois 60605
Phone: (312) 939-3330
Fax: (312) 663-3557

Printed in the United States of America

Contents

FOREWORD

It's not about the destination…it's about the journey. Nothing could better describe our 2006 season.

Our journey actually began in 1997 when I assumed ownership of the team. My goal was to achieve my family's dream of building a championship team and bringing the Lombardi Trophy home to Indiana.

To build the team, we needed an architect and I knew there was no one better than Bill Polian. In Bill's first draft in 1998, we picked Peyton Manning. The final part of our championship foundation fell into place when Tony Dungy signed on as our head coach.

Under the leadership of this trio, we began our journey. With drive, determination and discipline, we charted our course. We fielded the team carefully, but not always with the obvious picks. Our scouting staff somehow has always managed to find those "diamonds in the rough" that our veteran coaches develop into talent for our team.

At the same time, our front office grew the sponsor base and worked to achieve consistent sell-outs so we could fund our team. Our fan base grew and soon represented not just Indianapolis, but all of Indiana.

Like many successful journeys, ours was beset with tragedy. As families protect each other during difficult times, our team came together and supported one another through those valleys.

We started the 2006 season with strength and promise. Toward the end of the season, we hit some bumps but we never gave up. We didn't listen to those who wrote us off. We never stopped believing that this would be our year…that this was our chance.

After we won our first playoff game at home against Kansas City, Coach Dungy said, "The first game in the playoffs is the hardest." I knew he was right; we had cleared the first hurdle.

But then we had to face Baltimore in their stadium. It would be a tough environment, more so than usual. Our team took a "business as usual" approach to the game and managed to stay incredibly focused, despite the distractions.

When the Patriots beat the Chargers giving us home field advantage for the AFC Championship game, I let out a whoop. Now the scene was set. Our archrival was coming to our stadium for the showdown. Our win over the Patriots made history for our team and our city and sent us to Miami for Super Bowl XLI.

There's nothing better in the NFL than your first Super Bowl win as an owner. My family and I share this win with many people who made it happen: our entire franchise and their families, our sponsors and season ticket holders, our fans, our city and our state.

The journey was historic and the destination…it was sweet! **XLI**

Jim Irsay
Owner and CEO
Indianapolis Colts

Colts Owner and CEO Jim Irsay accepts the Vince Lombardi Trophy on behalf of Colts fans everywhere.

Sunday, February 4, 2007

WORLD CHAMPIONS

Patience, Perseverance Give Colts First Super Bowl Victory in 36 Years

All season, they came back.

All season, they overcame odds.

And throughout that improbable, memorable, dramatic, roller-coaster season, these were the constants for the Colts:

Persistence. Patience. Perseverance.

Think of it:

Could they have really won the Super Bowl any other way?

The Colts (16-4), after allowing the quickest score in Super Bowl history, overcame first-half deficits of seven and eight points, taking the lead by the end of a sloppy first half. They extended the lead in the third quarter and pulled away for a 29-17 victory over the Chicago Bears (15-4) Sunday night in Super Bowl XLI in front of 74,512 at Dolphin Stadium.

The Colts, a playoff team five consecutive seasons and in seven of the last eight seasons, won their first Super Bowl in their 23-year history in Indianapolis, and their first since winning Super Bowl V as the Baltimore Colts.

Indianapolis Colts . . .

World Champions.

"In years past, when we've come up short, it's been disappointing," said Colts quarterback Peyton Manning, who was named the game's Most Valuable Player after completing 25 of 38 passes for 247 yards and a touchdown with an interception.

"We've found a way to learn from those losses, and been better for it. It's nice when you put in a lot of hard work and you're able to cap it off with a championship. . . .

"We've really tried to enjoy the journey. It's nice to be able to complete it with a championship."

Indianapolis Colts . . .

World Champions.

"Our guys just kept saying, 'We're going to continue to fight – we're not going to be denied,'" said Colts Head Coach Tony Dungy, who became the first African-American Head Coach to win a Super Bowl.

"That heart will take you a long way."

It wasn't always pretty on a rainy night in South Florida,

Super Bowl XLI

Score by Quarters	1	2	3	4	Score
Indianapolis Colts	6	10	6	7	29
Chicago Bears	14	0	3	0	17

Manning maintained his focus in the first Super Bowl ever played in a downpour.

AP/Wide World

but as was the case throughout the 2006 season, the Colts were gutsy. They made plays when they had to, too.

"This is great for (Colts Owner and Chief Executive Officer) Jim (Irsay), great for Tony, great for the organization," Colts President Bill Polian said. "This is just outstanding for the city. What an outstanding bunch of guys. They wouldn't take no for an answer.

"They didn't believe any of the criticism. They listened to one voice. They kept playing hard and believing in what Tony told them, and they got it done."

A defense maligned throughout much of the season stifled the Bears for the last three quarters, holding the Bears to 265 yards and coming up with turnovers at crucial times.

Rookie Joseph Addai rushed for 77 yards on 19 carries and set a Super Bowl reception record for a running back with 10 catches for 66 yards.

An offense that was once called soft ran effectively against one of the NFL's best defenses. Colts running back Dominic Rhodes rushed for 113 yards on 21 carries and the Colts outrushed the Bears 191-111.

A team that lost four of its last seven regular-season games won the Super Bowl for the first time in NFL history.

An indoor, "dome" team won in the rain.

"As Tony said, we buried virtually everything tonight," Polian said. "We're built to play in a dome indoors. We

World Champions

Dwight Freeney dives for a fumble recovery in the first quarter.

Bob Sanders delivers a hit on Chicago running back Cedric Benson, forcing one of five Chicago turnovers.

can't play in bad weather. We can't play on grass. We can't stop the run. We can't play against people who are bigger and tougher than we are. We're too small. Peyton Manning can't win the big one. Tony Dungy can't win the big one."

All were criticisms of the Colts in the past.

All disappeared on Sunday night.

"To finally get that championship, man – it's the best feeling," Colts defensive tackle Raheem Brock said.

Making their first Super Bowl appearance in 36 years, the Colts struggled at times early, falling behind, 14-6, but outscored the Bears 23-3 in the final three quarters.

The Colts rallied from the eight-point deficit to take a 16-14 halftime lead, and after three quarters, they led 22-

17. Early in the fourth quarter, Colts cornerback Kelvin Hayden intercepted Bears quarterback Rex Grossman.

Hayden's 56-yard return down the left sideline all-but clinched a Super Bowl title Manning later called "years in the making."

And as was the case all season, nothing came easy for the Colts.

Bears returner Devin Hester, projected throughout the week as a key to the game, took the opening kickoff near the sideline, and returned it 92 yards for the first return of a game-opening kickoff in the 41-year history of the game.

World Champions

Manning and the Colts dominated the Bears in time of possession with a 38:04 to 21:56 advantage.

The Colts pulled to within one point when Manning passed 53 yards for a touchdown to wide receiver Reggie Wayne with 6:50 remaining in the quarter, but the Colts didn't get the hold down and the extra point failed.

That made it 7-6, and after an exchange of fumbles, Bears running back Thomas Jones' 52-yard run moved the Bears to the Colts 5.

On 3rd-and-goal from the 4, Grossman (20 of 28, 165 yards, one touchdown, two interceptions) threw to wide receiver Muhsin Muhammad for a 14-6 Bears lead with 4:34 remaining in the period.

If the first quarter was sloppy and strange, the second quarter was, too, but during it, the Colts rallied from an

Kelvin Hayden returns a fourth-quarter interception 56 yards for a touchdown to put the Colts ahead 29-17.

eight-point deficit to take a 16-14 lead.

The Colts cut the lead to 14-9 on a 29-yard field goal by Adam Vinatieri with 11:17 remaining in the second quarter.

Indianapolis held Chicago without a first down on its next possession. Taking possession at their 42-yard line, the Colts used seven plays to drive 58 yards, taking a 16-14 lead when veteran running back Dominic Rhodes ran for a 1-yard touchdown on 2nd-and-goal.

The Colts, who held Chicago without a first down in the

World Champions

Dominic Rhodes scores a second-quarter touchdown to give the Colts a 16-14 lead the club would not relinquish. Rhodes rushed for 113 yards on 21 carries.

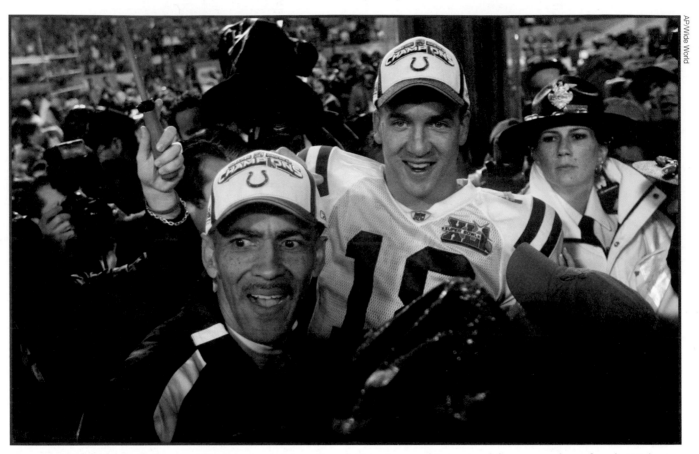

Manning and Dungy celebrate together after the Colts beat the Bears 29-17.

second quarter, had a chance to extend their lead on the final drive of the half, but Vinatieri missed wide left from 36 yards on the final play of the second quarter.

The Colts dominated the first half statistically, outgaining the Bears, 257-95, and producing 14 first downs to three for the Bears. The Colts finished with a 430-265 total-yardage advantage.

Each team committed three turnovers in the half, with the Bears losing three fumbles and the Colts losing two. Manning also threw a first-half interception.

Twice in the first half one team fumbled with the opponent recovering only to fumble the ball away on the game's next play.

Hester's kickoff return was the first time in Super

Bowl history a kick had been returned for a touchdown on the game's first play.

Afterward, as he addressed the team after the game, Dungy joked that while he knew there would be storms in the game, he didn't know they would come on the game's first play.

Minutes later, Dungy – long one of the most respected, classiest coaches in the NFL – was still speaking to the gathered media. He not only had become the first African-American to coach an NFL team to a world championship, he further solidified

World Champions

Anthony "Booger" McFarland is part of a Colts defensive line that flourished in the post-season, allowing only 83 rushing yards per game.

himself as one of the great coaches of his era. He has coached nine playoff teams in 11 seasons, and in five seasons with the Colts, his teams never have failed to make the playoffs.

The victory Sunday night put Dungy in other elite company, making him the third person to win a Super Bowl as a head coach and a player.

The victory as a player came with the 1978 Steelers and was sweet, Dungy said.

The victory Sunday night . . .

Well, the victory Sunday night was different, he said, meaningful in different ways, from a different perspective, one he said he'll never forget.

"Winning as a coach, you see the whole organization," Dungy said. "You see how hard everyone works – our scouting department, our personnel department,

Dungy and the Colts gave Indianapolis its first World Championship ever.

our front office, our equipment men, our trainers . . .

"I know what everybody put into it. I feel a lot more pride as a head coach because you understand how tough it is. It's a different feeling.

"I'm just so proud of our organization all together."

Minutes later, in the crowded Colts locker room, Dungy delivered a similar speech to the team.

"We hung tough, and everybody did their job," Dungy told the team. "When everybody does their job, it's a beautiful thing to watch. You're champions. We brought it back to Indianapolis."

Indianapolis Colts . . .

World Champions. **XLI**

Cato June and his teammates kept the Bears out of the end zone after the first quarter and allowed just 17 points in the game.

SUPER BOWL XLI STATISTIC

	Colts	Bears
1st Downs	24	11
Rushing	12	3
Passing	11	8
Penalty	1	0
3rd-Down Conversions	8-18	3-10
4th-Down Conversions	0-1	0-1
Punts-Average	4-40.5	5-45.2
Return Yards	225	147
Punts-Returns	3-42	1-3
Kickoffs-Returns	4-89	6-138
Int.-Returns	2-94	1-6
Penalties-Yards	6-40	4-35
Fumbles-Lost	2-2	4-3
Time Of Pos.	38:04	21:56
Total Net Yards	430	265
Total Plays	81	48
Average Gain	5.3	5.5
Net Yards Rushing	191	111
Rushes	42	19
Avg. Per Rush	4.5	5.8
Net Yards Passing	239	154
Comp.-Att.	25-38	20-28
Yards Per Pass	6.1	5.3
Sacked-Yards Lost	1-8	1-11
Had Intercepted	1	2
Touchdowns	3	2
Rushing	1	0
Passing	1	1
Other	1	1
Extra Points	2-3	2-2
Other	0-1	0-0
Red Zone Efficiency	1-6-17%	1-1-100%
Goal To Go Efficiency	1-2-50%	1-1-100%
Safeties	0	0

The Colts received a warm welcome downtown after bringing Indianapolis its first Super Bowl Trophy.

BIG-TIME PLAYER, BIG-TIME MOMENT

Manning-Led Drive Puts Colts in Super Bowl

Tony Dungy said what Peyton Manning didn't.

It was mixed in with the plethora of post-game quotes following the Colts 38-34 victory over the New England Patriots in the AFC Championship Game at the RCA Dome.

Minutes later, Manning–the Colts two-time Most Valuable Player and a seven-time Pro Bowl quarterback–would stand in the same place and say the moment wasn't about getting any monkey off his back, and that it wasn't about him at all.

Dungy, the Colts head coach, said the victory certainly wasn't about one player, but when discussing Manning, he made this much clear: Manning is a clutch player, always has been.

And if this performance wasn't necessary to prove that, it should provide sufficient evidence to support it.

"Peyton Manning's a great player," Dungy said after Manning completed 27 of 47 passes for 349 yards and a touchdown to help the Colts to their first Super Bowl appearance in 36 seasons.

"Anybody who doesn't know that doesn't know much about football."

Throughout much of the week leading up to the game, much of the media's attention focused on the Colts past playoff losses.

The Colts have made the playoffs seven of the past eight seasons, but until this win, had not reached the Super Bowl during their tenure in Indianapolis. Twice the Colts had lost road playoff games to the Patriots–24-14 in the AFC Championship Game following the 2003 season, and 20-3 in a Divisional Playoff following the 2004 season.

Those losses were talked about often, as was the disappointing 21-18 loss to the Pittsburgh Steelers in an AFC Divisional Playoff last season.

Manning, in his ninth NFL season, discussed the importance of the win a few days after the game, saying, "Certainly, the more you play, the longer you play–being in your ninth year - you realize you probably won't get many opportunities," Manning said. "When you have one, you want to be able to take advantage of it."

After a slow start against the Patriots, Manning took full advantage.

He struggled at times in the first half, and early in the second quarter—his lone interception of the game was returned 39 yards for a touchdown by Patriots cornerback Asante Samuel.

It took a heroic effort to overcome the Patriots, and Manning delivered in the clutch with a late fourth-quarter drive.

In the second half, Manning completed 14 of 23 passes for 225 yards and a touchdown with no interceptions for a passer rating of 108.1.

The Colts had possession eight times in the second half. Four of the drives ended in touchdowns, one with a field goal and two with punts.

The eighth possession ended with Manning kneeling for his first AFC Championship Game victory, but afterward, he said he felt no vindication after years of criticism for not making the Super Bowl.

"I just don't play that card," Manning said. "I thought this game was about two really good football teams and certainly the history we've had with this team. I can remember the disappointment three years ago when we lost up there to New England in the AFC Championship.

"That's been the number one question I've been asked so far. I don't get into monkeys and vindication. I just don't play that card. I know how hard I worked this week to get ready for these guys and it's always nice when you put that hard work to use and get a win."

On the Colts final drive, Manning completed three of four passes for 57 yards, and on 3rd-and-2 from the Patriots 3, Manning handed off to rookie running back Joseph Addai, who ran through the back of the end zone for the Colts first lead of the game.

Manning led the offense to touchdowns in four of the Colts eight second-half possessions.

"I don't know if you're supposed to pray for stuff like that, but I said a little prayer there," Manning said. "I'll say one thing about our last drive. There's no question–and it came from Coach Dungy–that we wanted to score a touchdown on that last drive. We did not want to score too fast once we got down there because you do not want to give Tom Brady that much time."

If Manning didn't use his post-championship forum to respond to years of criticism and doubters, his teammates said he could be excused for feeling at least some vindication.

"I hope it shuts everybody up," Colts center Jeff Saturday said. "He has worked so hard. He works as hard as anybody in this league. He does what's right and he shows up and he does his work."

Said Colts wide receiver Reggie Wayne, "He's been through a lot. A lot of criticism has been dealt to him. People have said he can't win the big games. I feel like I've been part of a lot of big games and we've come through and won and put on a good show. I'm happy for him. He deserves it. I'm happy for Coach Dungy and (Colts Owner and Chief Executive Officer) Jim Irsay and the city. I'm happy for everybody." **XLI**

Peyton Manning

Manning finished another stellar regular season by completing 362 of 557 pass attempts for 4,397 yards and 31 TDs with only nine interceptions.

A HISTORICAL TIME

Dungy Honored to be Part of History at Super Bowl XLI

Tony Dungy was ready for the deluge.

And yes, although he hadn't been to a Super Bowl as a participant in nearly three decades, he knew very well the week before the game would be a deluge.

It started moments after the Colts beat the New England Patriots in the AFC Championship Game. Dungy, the Colts head coach, received the question he anticipated considering the events of the day.

The topic was that he and his close friend, Chicago Bears Head Coach Lovie Smith, would be the first African-American head coaches to coach in the Super Bowl.

Dungy requested the question be delayed, so that he could focus on the moment.

The following day, it came again, and Dungy said he knew it would come often as the Colts and Bears descended into Miami for Super Bowl XLI.

And to Dungy, that's OK.

Because while he said it would be preferable if minority head coaches were no longer an issue in professional and college football, Dungy also said the reality is still different, that there is still progress to be made, still times when the issue needs a national stage.

And this much is true, too:

Dungy said he was proud, and aware of the moment's significance.

Mostly, he said, he was humbled.

"I'm just honored to be in this position, No. 1," Dungy said as the AFC Champion Colts (15-4) prepared to play the NFC Champion Chicago Bears (15-3) in Super Bowl XLI at Dolphin Stadium in Miami Gardens, Florida on Sunday, February 4 at 6:25 p.m.

"No. 2, it makes me think about the guys who were in the league when I came in."

That was 1981, 25 seasons ago, a time when African-American players made up a major part of NFL rosters. At the time, there were 28 teams in the NFL.

There were 14 African-American assistants, and no head coaches.

"But there were some good guys, some guys who were exceptional, but who never really got the chance to do what Lovie and I got to do," Dungy said. "You think about those guys. You think about Sherman Lewis and Jimmy Raye and Earnel Durden and Lionel Taylor – they could have taken a team to a Super Bowl, but never got the opportunity.

"We (he and Smith) feel like we've been blessed and gotten that. I think about my generation of kids who watched Super Bowls and never really saw African-American coaches and didn't maybe necessarily think about the fact that you could be the coach."

Head Coach Tony Dungy celebrates the franchise's first title in 36 years.

True Blue

Much has changed in 25 years, and since he joined the Pittsburgh Steelers as a defensive assistant, Dungy has been at the forefront of the progress.

He became the Steelers' defensive coordinator in 1984, and 12 years later – after stints as the Kansas City Chiefs' defensive backs coach and the Minnesota Vikings' defensive coordinator – he became the NFL's third African-American head coach of the modern era when he was hired by the Tampa Bay Buccaneers.

Art Shell became the first African-American NFL head coach since Fritz Pollard coached the Akron Pros in 1921 when he was hired by the Oakland Raiders in 1989. Since Shell, Dennis Green (Minnesota, Arizona), Dungy (Tampa Bay, Indianapolis), Herman Edwards (New York Jets, Kansas City), Smith (Chicago), Marvin Lewis (Cincinnati), Romeo Crennel (Cleveland) and Ray Rhodes (Green Bay, Philadelphia) are the only African-Americans to have been NFL head coaches.

The Steelers this past week hired Mike Tomlin as the first African-American head coach in franchise history.

This past season, there were a record seven African American head coaches and 197 assistants, including seven assistant head coaches.

Of the six current African-American NFL head coaches – Dungy, Lewis, Edwards, Tomlin, Smith and Crennel – Dungy hired three: Smith, Edwards and Tomlin.

"My thought was, the only way we're going to change that is the people who have the opportunity to change it are going to have to," Dungy said. "Fortunately, I was put in the position where I had the opportunity to change it. Your thought is not just hiring black coaches, but getting good coaches and getting good people into the league and giving them a chance to come into the league.

"For me, it was bringing good coaches into the league, but in my heart of hearts, bringing good African-American coaches into the league."

He has continued to do that in Indianapolis, where his staff features eight African-American coaches: assistant head coach/quarterbacks Jim Caldwell, special assistant to the Head Coach/Defensive Backs Leslie Frazier, strength and conditioning assistant Rich Howell, running backs coach Gene Huey, defensive coordinator Ron Meeks, defensive quality control coach Diron Reynolds, tight ends coach Ricky Thomas and defensive backs coach Alan Williams.

Caldwell has interviewed for several head jobs in recent seasons, including Arizona earlier this month. Dungy often has spoken of Caldwell as a future NFL head coach.

"Hopefully, young kids now can say, 'Hey, I might be the coach someday,' so that's special," Dungy said. "That's something I thought about when I was an assistant and when I got the job at Tampa. It was important to me to get some guys into the pipeline.

"I'm very, very proud I was able to hire Herm, and hire Lovie and hire Mike Tomlin. Those guys are going to have a chance to do it also."

Getting the chance to give others the chance wasn't easy, Dungy said. When he was the defensive coordinator under Green at Minnesota from 1992-1995, he interviewed for several head jobs, including one with Green Bay when he was told the team was looking for an offensive assistant with head-coaching experience.

Dungy, a defensive coach, never had been a head coach.

Race also played a factor at times, Dungy said.

"I know, for me, I had a couple of situations in interviews where a guy would ask me about what kind of staff I'd put together—who was this guy, was he white or black, how many black coaches are you going to have?" Dungy said. "It startles you a little bit.

"That was many years ago, but it happened. I had a general manager I respect really well tell me if I wanted to move up in this business I needed to shave my beard. I was about 28 or 29 years old. He said, 'People are looking for a certain style of person.'

"Fortunately, I was working for (Steelers owner) Dan Rooney at the time and he told that wasn't something I even needed to worry about."

Continued Dungy, "I didn't have that many (interviews) - not as many as people thought - and the ones that I had I thought were very, very sincere. But when you would get questions like that, where you could see people were concerned about things that didn't really relate to football, I could tell we had a ways to go."

Looking back now, Dungy said he wished he might have ended those interviews sooner.

"I never did, but after a couple of them were over, I felt I should have," Dungy said. "At the time, I just tried to answer the questions honestly.

"We've come a long way and I think we're past that stage."

Overall, Dungy said there has been progress. And Dungy said he doesn't necessarily think NFL owners ever actively strove to prevent African-Americans from becoming head coaches.

"I don't fault people, necessarily," Dungy said. "I think we're all a product of our environment and our past. I know when people were looking for coaches at one time, you just had to go on what you'd seen before. You didn't see a lot of African-American coaches.

"You'd seen a certain style. You'd seen a certain type of person, a coach that looked a certain way, a person that came from a certain background. I think that was part of it."

Over the last decade, Dungy has helped change that perception. He has been one of the most successful head coaches of this or any era. In 1996, he took over as the head coach of the Tampa Bay Buccaneers, and a year later, he led the Bucs to their first playoff appearance in 15 seasons.

Two years after that, they were in the NFC Championship Game. In 11 seasons as an NFL head coach, his teams have made nine playoff appearances and three appearances in conference championship games.

In his five seasons as head coach, the Colts have made five playoff appearances and won four consecutive AFC South titles.

Early in his career, he said this week, he felt a pressure to succeed–not because of a fear that others would never get a chance if he failed, but because others would get a chance more quickly should he succeed.

Succeed he did, and for that reason, he said he knows there will be a deluge of questions in the weeks before the Super Bowl. That's fine, he said, because discussing it may raise awareness.

And if that means a deluge for a week, Dungy said that's OK if it means progress and opportunity.

"We'll probably talk this subject to death in the next two weeks," Dungy accurately predicted. "It probably will get to the point where we'll feel like we've heard it for 100 years. I think when you look at the last five or six years, and how many times Herman has been to the playoffs, and what Marvin Lewis has done in Cincinnati and what Lovie has done in Chicago — hopefully, we're getting go that point where people realize, 'Hire the best person, they're going to do a good job.'

"Players are going to respond to coaches whoever they are." **XLI**

Sunday, January 21, 2007

SUPER BOWL-BOUND!

Colts Rally from 18-Point Deficit to Beat New England in
AFC Championship Game

As far as Tony Dungy was concerned, it couldn't have been more perfect.

Fitting, the Colts head coach called it.

And indeed it was.

Playing their longtime nemesis, playing at home, playing with a chance to go to the Super Bowl for the first time in more than three decades, the Colts fell behind by 18 points in front of 57,433 fans in the AFC Championship Game at the RCA Dome Sunday night.

Then, the Colts fought back.

They kept fighting.

And then they fought some more.

When it was over, after Colts quarterback Peyton Manning threw his final clutch pass in the face of the New England Patriots' relentless defense, after running back Joseph Addai's game-winning touchdown run with a minute remaining, after cornerback Marlin Jackson's last-minute interception . . .

When all that was over, the Colts quest for the Super Bowl was over, too.

Colts 38, Patriots 34.

Indianapolis Colts . . . AFC Champions.

"That sounds good," Manning said moments after completing 27 of 47 passes for 349 yards and a touchdown. "It really does."

The Colts, the four-time defending AFC South champions, made the Super Bowl in the most storybook fashion possible, beating a team that eliminated them from the playoffs following the 2003 and 2004 seasons.

They did it by outscoring the Patriots 32-13 in the second half.

They did it with the largest comeback in the 37-year history of AFC and NFC Championship Games.

They did it with a memorable, storybook drive, 80 yards on seven plays in 1:17, going ahead with Addai's 3-yard touchdown run with 1:00 remaining.

They did it with clutch play from Manning, the National Football League's Most Valuable Player in 2003 and 2004, and a player who listened all week to still more questions about his ability to win in clutch, playoff situations.

New England Patriots at Indianapolis Colts

Score by Quarters	1	2	3	4	Score
New England Patriots	7	14	7	6	34
Indianapolis Colts	3	3	15	17	38

Manning produced a vintage performance in the AFC Championship Game game.

"I think it was great for Peyton to get to the Super Bowl with a drive like that," Colts Head Coach Tony Dungy said.

They also did it with a clutch play from a defense that was maligned throughout the season, with Jackson clinching the game with an interception with 16 seconds remaining.

And they did it on the same day that the Chicago Bears beat the New Orleans Saints to qualify for the Super Bowl from the NFC. That victory means Dungy and his longtime friend, Bears Head Coach Lovie Smith, will be the first African-American head coaches in the Super Bowl.

But that story, Dungy said, is for later.

Because Sunday night was about celebrating the Colts, and about celebrating the accomplishment of a five-year dream, one that began shortly after the 2001 season, when Colts Owner Jim Irsay hired him as head coach.

"More than that today, this is about Indianapolis and the Colts and our team," Dungy said. "We're excited about that."

Since Dungy's 2002 hiring, the Colts have made the playoffs five consecutive seasons, and along with the Patriots are the only team to win four consecutive division titles.

But until Sunday night, a Super Bowl berth had eluded the Colts.

And for a half, it appeared to many it might eluded them again.

The Colts fell behind 21-3 in the first half, and still trailed 21-6 at halftime.

Then came one of the most remarkable comebacks in NFL postseason history, a comeback certain to make the game "an instant classic," as Manning called it.

The Colts cut the lead to 21-13 with a 1-yard sneak by

Manning on the first drive of the third quarter, then tied it on the ensuing series with a 1-yard pass from Manning to defensive tackle Dan Klecko, acquired just before the season off waivers from New England.

After that, it was back and forth into history.

The Patriots scored on a controversial 6-yard pass from two-time Super Bowl Most Valuable Player Tom Brady to wide receiver Jabar Gaffney, but the Colts responded with a 67-yard, seven-play drive to tie it early in the fourth quarter.

On that drive, Colts center Jeff Saturday recovered a fumble in the end zone to tie the game, 28-28.

The teams traded field goals in the middle of the final period, and with 3:49 remaining, Patriots kicker Stephen Gostkowski's 43-yard field goal gave New England a 34-31 lead.

Then came a drive for which Manning and the Colts long will be remembered.

On 2nd-and-10 from the Colts 31, Manning threw deep to reserve tight end Bryan Fletcher, who caught a 32-yard bomb for a first down at the Patriots 37.

A play later, Manning threw 14 yards to wide receiver Reggie Wayne, and the Colts moved 12 yards closer after a roughing the passer penalty on the Patriots.

Three runs later, on 3rd-and-2 from the Patriots 3, Manning handed off to Addai. A gaping hole opened in the middle and after the point after by kicker Adam Vinatieri, the Colts led, 38-34.

All that was left was to stop the Patriots, but Brady - one of the NFL's all-time postseason clutch quarterbacks - had a minute remaining and two timeouts.

The Patriots reached the Colts 45. Twenty-four seconds remaining.

Brady's pass on 1st-and-10 sailed toward tight end Benjamin Watson.

Jackson cut in front of the pass. Interception.

Dallas Clark led the Colts with six receptions for 137 yards against New England.

Game over, and the RCA Dome crowd - on edge and raucous throughout - celebrated, shaking the stands and sending the Colts players, coaches and personnel into euphoria.

"It's a good feeling because of how hard we worked this season," Manning said. "I know how hard I've worked, how hard our team has worked. It's always nice to see hard work rewarded, you know, with a great opportunity to go down to Miami."

The Patriots, 5-1 all-time in the AFC Championship Game, took a 7-3 lead at the end of the first quarter, scoring their first touchdown when guard Logan Mankins fell on a fumble by Brady in the end zone for a seven-point lead.

Vinatieri's 42-yard field goal on the ensuing drive cut the Patriots' lead to four, 7-3, with 38 seconds remaining in the quarter.

The Patriots, Super Bowl champions following the 2001, 2003 and 2004 seasons, scored two second-quarter touchdowns in a span of less than one minute to extend the lead to 18 points.

The Patriots, who led 7-3 after the first quarter, took a 14-3 lead with 10:18 remaining before halftime when running back Corey Dillon scored on a 7-yard run.

On the ensuing series, Patriots cornerback Asante Samuel intercepted Manning, and after a 39-yard return, the Patriots led 21-3 with 9:25 remaining in the second quarter.

Late in the quarter, the Colts drove 80 yards on 15 plays, cutting the lead to 15 points when Vinatieri kicked a 26-yard field goal seven seconds before halftime.

Manning, the NFL's Most Valuable Player in 2003 and 2004, completed 13 of 24 passes for 124 yards and no touchdowns with an interception in the first half for a passer rating of 51.4.

Brady completed 8 of 12 passes for 91 yards and no touchdowns with no interceptions in the first half.

The Patriots outgained the Colts, 170-144, in the first half, but after trailing 21-6 at halftime, the Colts drove 76 yards on 14 plays, with Manning scoring on a 1-yard run to pull the Colts to within eight, 21-13.

After holding the Patriots without a first down on their ensuing possession, Manning drove the Colts 76 yards on six plays, pulling Indianapolis to within two - 21-19 - on a 1-yard pass to defensive tackle Dan Klecko.

The Colts then tied it, 21-21, when Manning threw a two-point conversion to wide receiver Marvin Harrison.

Patriots cornerback Ellis Hobbs returned the ensuing kickoff 80 yards to the Colts 21, after which New England used five plays for the go-ahead touchdown.

That came when Brady evaded a heavy rush and threw a 6-yard touchdown pass to wide receiver Jabar Gaffney.

That put the Patriots ahead, 28-21, with 16:25 remaining, but as Dungy and Colts players said was the case throughout the game - even trailing by 18 to a team that had won three of the past five Super Bowls – there was no panic, no anger.

All there was, Dungy said, was a resolve to fight, to get to the Super Bowl, something that finally happened in an fashion Dungy said couldn't have been more fitting.

"Obviously, there's a lot of emotion in that locker room," Dungy said. "I could not be more proud of our guys. We had to do it the hard way. We had to go through a great champion and we got down 18 points to them and that's not easy.

"Our team went the hard way the whole year, but they hung tough and I'm so proud of them. I'm excited for our whole city, our whole organization, taking our team to the Super Bowl.

"Couldn't ask for a better way to end this part of our year." **XLI**

Marlin Jackson intercepted Tom Brady with 24 seconds remaining to clinch the AFC Championship Game.

Sunday, January 14, 2007

KICKING IT UP A NOTCH

Colts Beat Baltimore to Qualify for AFC Championship Game

The Colts had the blueprint.

They knew what it would take to win a playoff game on the road, against the National Football League's No. 1-ranked defense.

It would take big-time defense.

It would take toughness.

It would take patience.

The Colts (14-4), champions of the AFC South, showed all three, overcoming a hostile crowd and a dominant defense with a stifling defensive effort of their own. Kicker Adam Vinatieri converted all five of his field goal attempts and the Colts held the Baltimore Ravens (13-4) to 244 total yards and two field goals in a 15-6 victory in an AFC Divisional Playoff game in front of 71,162 at M&T Bank Stadium.

"A lot of people say, 'Throw the statistics out the window in the playoffs, and just get a win,'" said Colts quarterback Peyton Manning, who completed 15 of 30 passes for 170 yards and no touchdowns with two interceptions for a passer rating of 39.6. "But it's like we're the exception: 'The Colts passing yards were this, the rating was this.'

"I do kind of agree, that you do kind of have to throw (statistics) out the window and I don't think we should be the exception. You do whatever you can to try to make a couple of big third-down conversions, you take your field goals where you can."

Vinatieri converted field goals of 23, 42, 51, 48 and 35 yards, and the Colts defense – much-maligned throughout the season – forced four turnovers.

"Sometimes, you can win like that," said Vinatieri, now 8-for-8 on field goals in this year's postseason. "Sometimes, you score a bunch of points. Sometimes, you score a little bit.

"As long as you score more than they do, everybody's happy."

The Colts defense, which allowed 173 yards rushing a game during the regular season, held the Ravens to 83 yards rushing.

"We knew it was going to be a defensive game," Colts defensive tackle Raheem Brock said. "We knew it was going to be on us. We knew we had to exe-

Indianapolis Colts at Baltimore Ravens

Score by Quarters	1	2	3	4	Score
Indianapolis Colts	6	3	3	3	15
Baltimore Ravens	0	3	0	3	6

Adam Vinatieri hit five field goals at Baltimore to lead the Colts to a 15-6 victory.

cute the game plan.

"We went out there and executed it great. We knew what we were supposed to go and we came out with the win."

The Colts (14-4), who entered the playoffs as the No. 3 seed, advanced to the AFC Championship Game for the second time in four seasons. They will play the winner of Sunday's AFC Divisional Playoff game between the New England Patriots and San Diego Chargers in San Diego.

"It doesn't matter who we play," Colts linebacker Cato June said. "Everybody on both teams will be ready to play. We have guys in this locker room who have been that close before. We know what it feels like."

If the fourth-seeded Patriots (13-4) win, the title game will be held in Indianapolis at the RCA Dome, where the Colts are 9-0 this season.

If the top-seeded Chargers (14-2) win, the title game will be in San Diego.

"Whoever we play next week will be definitely the best team we've played all year," Colts middle linebacker Rob Morris said.

The Colts never have hosted an AFC title game since the team's 1984 move to Indianapolis.

"We'd love to have the game at home for our fans, but for us – we won at home last week and we won on the road this week," Colts Head Coach Tony Dungy said. "We lost at home last year. It really doesn't matter.

"We're going to play a great team, whoever we play, and we're going to be ready for them."

The Colts victory snapped a four-game road losing streak, and gave the Colts a 2-2 record under Dungy in divisional playoff games. The Colts beat Kansas City on the road in a divisional playoff following the 2003 season and lost in the round the past two seasons – at New England and at home against Pittsburgh.

The Ravens had entered the game with the NFL's best home record since 2000, winning 42 games and losing 14 in the regular season.

When Dungy discussed the Baltimore game this week, he talked of wanting a solid early effort, one that kept the Colts in the game. That's exactly what he got.

The Colts turned in a solid first-quarter defensive effort, shutting out the Ravens and allowing the offense to take a 6-0 lead. They got the same kind of defense the rest of the game, holding the Ravens 244 total yards.

"It's the playoffs, and you know going into the play-offs it doesn't matter anymore how many yards you give up," Colts safety Sanders said. "When you go into the playoffs, you have to take it as a whole new season. The regular season, it's over and it's done with.

"We're in the playoffs now. Every team is 0-0."

The Colts offense scored on five of 11 possessions, and while the Ravens were converting 2 of 11 third downs, the Colts converted 8 of 19.

The Colts had just four drives of five or more plays, but all ended in field goals.

"Offensively, we knew how it was going to be," Dungy said. "You're trying to get big plays and we got just enough of them. We missed a couple we were close on, but that's the way they force you to play and our defense answered the challenge.

"The defense knew it was going to be that type of game. We came up with a couple of takeaways and that helped us."

The Colts defense, maligned much of the season with the 32nd-ranked rushing defense in the NFL, was solid early in the first quarter, forcing a turnover, and ensuring positive field position on the Colts first two offensive possessions.

The Colts forced three turnovers – interceptions by

Robert Mathis had three tackles, one sack, one forced fumble and one fumble recovery to lead the Colts pass rush at Baltimore.

safety Jason David and cornerback Nick Harper – and linebacker Gary Brackett recovered an early turnover. The Ravens, who forced two turnovers, are 51-5 under Head Coach Brian Billick when they had a position turnover ratio, but 8-41 with a negative ratio.

The Colts drove 49 yards on 11 plays on their first drive, a series capped by a 23-yard field goal by Vinatieri.

Vinatieri gave the Colts a 6-0 lead on their next possession, kicking a 42-yard field goal three plays after Colts linebacker Gary Brackett recovered a fumble by Ravens tight end Todd Heap at the Baltimore 31.

Vinatieri then finished the Colts first-half scoring with a 51-yard field goal that bounced over the crossbar with 3:15 remaining in the second quarter.

That gave the Colts a six-point lead and capped a drive that began at the Ravens 1 after an interception by Colts safety Antoine Bethea.

Bethea's interception was the second Ravens turnover of the half.

The Colts lone first-half turnover came when safety

Ryan Lilja and the Colts offensive line led a 13-play, 47-yard fourth-quarter drive that took more than seven minutes to clinch a divisional playoff win at Baltimore.

Ed Reed intercepted Colts quarterback Peyton Manning at the Ravens 45 with 14:09 remaining in the quarter.

Bethea's interception stopped the ensuing Ravens drive.

Ravens kicker Matt Stover kicked a 40-yard field goal on the first play of the second quarter to cut a 6-0 Colts lead in half.

Vinatieri added a 48-yard field goal early in the second half to extend the Colts lead to 12-3, and Stover's 51-yard field goal with 13:03 remaining made it, 12-6, Colts.

With the title-game appearance on the line, Colts cornerback Nick Harper intercepted McNair in Colts territory in the fourth quarter. After an exchange of punts, the Colts offense then drained more than seven minutes from the clock on a game-clinching drive that ended with Vinatieri's final field goal. **XLI**

Colts vs Ravens

Ravens running backs Mike Anderson (above) and Jamal Lewis could only muster 71 rushing yards on 17 carries against the stout Colts defense.

Saturday, January 6, 2007

PERFECT STORM

Colts 23-8 Victory over Kansas City in Wild-Card Round
a Complete Game

There was, Tony Dungy said, no real mystery.

The difference between the Colts defense on Saturday and the Colts defense much of the regular season?

The reason it suddenly played so well?

The reason it was a fun, upbeat story after the Colts 23-8 victory over the Kansas City Chiefs in an AFC Wild-Card Playoff Saturday rather than the negative one it has been much of the season?

The reason was simple, Dungy said.

No big alterations in the game plan.

No pre-game speeches.

No big secrets.

"We really didn't change anything," Dungy said Sunday, a day after the Colts record-setting defensive day in front of a raucous, sold-out RCA Dome Saturday.

The Colts, who won their fourth consecutive AFC South title this season, advanced to their fourth AFC Divisional Playoff in the last four seasons with their victory over the Chiefs. The third-seeded Colts (13-4) will visit the second-seeded Baltimore Ravens (13-3) at M&T Bank Stadium Saturday at 4:30 p.m.

The Colts won in the Divisional Playoff Round following the 2003 season, beating the Kansas City Chiefs in Kansas City, Mo., 38-31, but lost in the round the last two seasons – losing at New England, 20-3, two seasons ago and at home to Pittsburgh, 21-18, last season.

"It really was a good win for us, one of those 'perfect-storm' kind of things," Dungy said Sunday during his weekly next-day news conference. "Everything just came together right. I thought we did play fast and play with a lot of energy. . . .

"We went in and played with the playoff energy you need. Now, our task is to forget that, put it out of our mind and try to duplicate that effort on the road against a really, really tough team."

On Saturday, the Colts advanced with a record-setting performance that surprised many NFL observers because the records were set by a defense that had struggled at times this season.

Kansas City Chiefs at Indianapolis Colts

Score by Quarters	1	2	3	4	Score
Kansas City Chiefs	0	0	8	0	8
Indianapolis Colts	6	3	7	7	23

The Colts defense produced four sacks and three takeaways, while holding the Chiefs without a first down for the first 42 minutes of the game.

The Colts, who entered the postseason ranked 32nd in the NFL against the run and 21st overall, set or tied three franchise-playoff records Saturday:

• 126 net yards allowed (old record: 139 against Cincinnati in 1970).
• 44 rushing yards allowed (old record: 56 against Cleveland in 1968).
• Seven first downs allowed (old record: seven against Cincinnati in 1970).

Players afterward said the Colts defense – maligned much of the season – didn't do much differently Sunday. They played better, they said, made fewer mistakes and played more fundamentally sound than they had in recent weeks.

Even the one major difference last week wasn't actually much of a difference, Dungy said.

The Colts kept their practice closed to the media last week, the first time since the week leading to a playoff victory over the Denver Broncos after the 2003 season they had done so.

That week, the Colts made a change offensively, playing center Jeff Saturday at guard and moving then-guard Tupe Peko to center.

This past week's big change? Dungy said there wasn't one.

"I closed practice because I wanted them (the Chiefs) to think we were changing something, to say, 'Hey, if they close practice maybe they're going to do something different.' Maybe (Chiefs Head Coach) Herm (Edwards) knows me a little bit too well for that.

"He probably didn't fall for that. (But) that was the theory behind it."

The victory Sunday kept the Colts perfect at home this season. After winning all eight games in the RCA Dome

Marvin Harrison caught two passes for 48 yards, including this 42-yard catch and run.

in the regular season, they are now 9-0 there this season.

The Colts, during Dungy's first four seasons, were one of the NFL's best road teams. From 2002 until the middle of this season, they were 28-8 on the road in the regular season and 29-11 including playoffs, but late this regular season, they lost four consecutive games on the road.

Their previous longest losing streak on the road under Dungy: two games.

The Colts this season beat three playoff teams on the road – the New York Jets, the New York Giants and the New England Patriots – and also beat another team that finished with a winning record, the Denver Broncos.

"We have a lot of guys who have played a lot of good

In the first playoff game of his career, Joseph Addai rushed 25 times for 122 yards and one touchdown.

road games here," Dungy said. "We've won in tough venues before. I don't think we fear going on the road. We just have to find a way to play at that high level. . . .

"We have, up until the last four times, been a pretty good road team. That's one of the things we've been proud of. We have to get that back."

The high level of Saturday's victory came because of what Dungy called a total team effort. Although quarterback Peyton Manning threw three interceptions, he also completed 30 of 38 passes for 268 yards and a 5-yard, game-clinching touchdown to wide receiver Reggie Wayne early in the fourth quarter.

Running back Joseph Addai, making his first NFL start, rushed for 126 yards and a touchdown on 25 carries.

The Colts outgained the Chiefs, 435-126, and had 28 first downs to seven for the Chiefs. The Colts also limited the Chiefs' kick return teams, allowing Kansas City an average starting position of the 21-

Raheem Brock and the defensive unit set the tone for the Colts against Kansas City, holding Larry Johnson to no gain on the first play of the game.

yard line on kickoffs.

It was a playoff-worthy effort, Dungy said, and one the Colts will have to not only repeat, but improve upon significantly next week in Baltimore.

"Our special teams and defense played with a speed we hope to exhibit all the time," Dungy said. "Offensively, we moved the ball very well and probably didn't finish drives as well as our guys would like. We had good execution for the most part. We did a lot of the things we wanted to do.

"We made some mistakes that in a real tight game come back to haunt you. We have to work to correct those. You can't have that happen. Otherwise, you're going home." **XLI**

Defensive Coordinator Ron Meeks guided a Colts defense that set club playoff records against Kansas City with only 44 rushing yards and 126 net yards allowed.

Sunday, September 10, 2006

STARTING IT RIGHT

Colts Beat New York Giants in Season Opener, 26-21

Peyton Manning wanted one thing made clear.

The whole Manning Bowl thing? Not his idea.

At a bowl game, the way Manning remembers it from his college days, "You get gear," he said, laughing late Sunday night.

There was no gear at the Colts 2006 regular-season opener Sunday night.

No travel bag.

No free T-shirt.

No commemorative watch.

What there was, actually, was what Manning and the Colts wanted more than anything from the 2006 regular-season opener. Because there was a victory, with the Colts beating the New York Giants, 26-21, in front of a nationally-television audience and 78,622 screaming fans at Giants Stadium.

"It was a different feeling out there," said Manning, who completed 25 of 41 passes for 276 yards and a touchdown with an interception.

He added, "The main thing at a bowl game is you get some gear, some bowl gear. Some sweat suits or some watches. I never saw that.

"I don't even use the term, 'Bowl.' I thought it was Colts versus Giants. It was two good teams. You've got a real Super Bowl contender over there."

The Colts won their season opener for the second consecutive season, and the seventh time in eight seasons. They have won the last three AFC South titles and have made the postseason each of the last four seasons.

"You can't win 12 or 13 until you win the first one," Colts three-time Pro Bowl defensive end Dwight Freeney said.

"The worst thing to do is lose the first one, then you've got a bunch of pressure on you to win the second game," Colts Pro Bowl center Jeff Saturday said. "That's really the way you look at it. The big thing is to come into a hostile environment, play a great football team – a playoff-type team – and get a victory.

"That shows a lot about our team and the goals we're trying to get done here."

But most notable to the national television audience was that the victory came in the first game in which

Indianapolis Colts at New York Giants

Score by Quarters	1	2	3	4	Score
Indianapolis Colts	3	13	0	10	26
New York Giants	0	7	7	7	21

Pro Bowl left tackle Tarik Glenn and the Colts offensive line led the league in 2006 in fewest sacks allowed with only 15.

two brothers have started against one another at quarterback in an NFL game, with Manning's younger brother, Eli, starting at quarterback for the Giants.

Eli Manning, in his third NFL season, completed 20 of 34 passes for 247 yards, rallying the Giants from a 13-0 deficit to within two points in the fourth quarter.

"I thought Eli played his butt off," Peyton Manning said.

Because of the brothers' high-profile – Peyton being a two-time NFL Most Valuable Player and the No. 1 overall selection in the 1998 NFL Draft and Eli being the No. 1 overall selection in the 2004 NFL Draft – the game received buildup unique for a season opener.

"The main thing is, the Colts beat the Giants tonight," Manning said.

The Colts did so by first taking a 13-0 first-half lead, then extending a 13-7 lead to 16-7 on a late first-half field goal by kicker Adam Vinatieri, who made all four field goal attempts in his first regular-season game with the Colts.

A 15-yard touchdown pass from Eli Manning to tight end Jeremy Shockey cut the Colts lead to 16-14 in the third quarter. And after Colts defensive end Robert Mathis recovered a fumble near midfield, Indianapolis drove 51 yards for a nine-point lead when veteran running back Dominic Rhodes scored on a 1-yard run.

That made it, 23-14, Colts, with 13:13 remaining.

But the Giants, opening defense of their NFC East title at home, were far from done. They drove 78 yards on 11 plays, cutting the lead to two on a 1-yard run by Brandon Jacobs with 8:01 remaining to set up a nail-biting finish.

The Giants then took possession after a Colts punt

Offensive Coordinator Tom Moore has guided an offense that has amassed 5,000-plus net yards in nine consecutive seasons, including three 6,000-plus yard seasons.

needing a field goal to take the lead. On 3rd-and-2 from their 18, Eli Manning completed a 19-yard pass to Tim Carter, who was called for offensive pass interference against cornerback Nick Harper, nullifying the gain.

Harper intercepted Manning on the ensuing play. Vinatieri's fourth field goal – a 32-yarder with 1:12 remaining – gave the Colts a 26-21 lead.

The Giants' final drive ended on their 46-yard line as time expired.

The Giants rushed for 186 yards on 28 carries, with Tiki Barber – who finished second in the NFL in rushing last season – rushing for 118 yards on 10 carries.

"I don't know that they tried to grind us down," Dungy said. "They've got a great back. They gave him the ball. We didn't play as good a run defense as we need to, but if I had Tiki Barber, I'd run him, too."

The Colts offense, as it had been throughout the pre-season, was efficient early Sunday, scoring on its first four possessions and not punting until just over six minutes remained in the third quarter.

"It felt lot like Baltimore last year," Colts wide receiver Reggie Wayne said, referring to a 24-7 victory over the Ravens in the 2005 season opener. "It doesn't matter how you get the win. Just get it done."

Despite the nine-point lead, the Colts were outgained at halftime, 226-215, with Barber rushing for 54 yards on 10 carries. The Giants had 98 yards on 13 carries – a 7.5-yard average – at the half.

"You want to start off the season playing well," Colts linebacker Cato June said. "We didn't play well, but we got the win. Now we know we can win and not be playing that well, but we need to play well so later on in the season we're not making those same mistakes."

The Colts took a 3-0 lead with a 26-yard field goal by Vinatieri midway through the first quarter. That capped a 17-play, 58-yard drive, and one possession late, Vinatieri's 32-yard field goal pushed Indianapolis' lead to 6-0.

Indianapolis continued to control momentum early, with Giants kicker Jay Feely missing a 40-yard field goal with 7:12 remaining and the Colts taking possession and driving to a two-possession lead.

Taking possession on their 30, the Colts drove 70 yards on 10 plays, with Manning throwing two yards on 3rd-and-2 from the Giants 2 for a 13-0 Indianapolis lead.

The Giants regained momentum shortly thereafter, with Eli Manning passing 34 yards to wide receiver Plaxico Burress with 32 seconds remaining in the half. Burress caught the ball reaching over Harper to cut the Colts lead to six, 13-7.

"Defensively, we just weren't sharp," Dungy said. "I know a lot of it had to do with New York really studying us. They did a good job and they had some good stuff up for us. But we didn't tackle as well as we needed to and we didn't play as well as we're going to need to as we carry on this year."

Peyton Manning then drove the Colts 31 yards in five plays, allowing Vinatieri to kick a 48-yard field goal – his third field goal of the half without a miss – to give the Colts a 16-7 halftime lead.

The Giants continued to control the momentum in the third quarter, maintaining possession for nearly nine minutes after the second-half kickoff.

Eli Manning's 15-yard touchdown to Shockey cut the lead to two with 7:10 remaining in the quarter, setting the stage for a memorable finish in a game Dungy and Manning each said afterward they were glad to be over, and particularly pleased to have won.

"They have an outstanding team and there was a lot of emotion in the stadium tonight, and a lot of energy all week," Dungy said. "We didn't play our best, but we were able to get a win. I thought our offense did a good job of making enough plays for us and keeping time of possession.

"We're happy with the win. I think our defense will get sharper as we go. They've got an excellent football team and we're 1-0, so we're excited about it."

Said Saturday, "The way the media hyped it up, it was a Manning-Manning type thing. There was a lot of hype for the game, but the reality is whatever team played better tonight was going to win the ball game. I'm glad we got the win. They're a great football team in New York. We're just glad we got the victory." **XLI**

Sunday, September 17, 2006

AVOIDING THE TRAP

Colts Dominate Early, Beat Texans in AFC South Opener

So much for the "Trap Game" theory.

The Colts had a much-hyped, nationally-televised game in the season opener last week. Next week, they will play the Jacksonville Jaguars, a team many expect to contend for the division title.

On Sunday, the Colts played the Houston Texans, a team that never had beaten the Colts and a team that entered the game as heavy underdogs.

A trap game? A difficult week to maintain focus?

An upset in the making?

Hardly.

With the offense working efficiently, and with the defense creating chaos early, Indianapolis (2-0 in 2006) dominated throughout the 2006 home opener, taking a 14-point first-half lead en route to a 43-24 over the Houston Texans (0-2) in front of 56,614 on Sunday afternoon at the RCA Dome.

"You can call this game a trap game, but I think we came out practiced well with a sense of urgency," Colts defensive tackle Montae Reagor said. "We came out and jumped on this ballclub early.

"We did the things we had to do to put them in the hole, to make them one-dimensional. We did what we had to do to put us in a position to win."

The victory gave the Colts a 21-4 record in the AFC South since its 2002 inception. The Colts, the division champions the past three seasons, have won 10 consecutive games against division opponents.

They will play host to the Jaguars (1-0), the division runners-up the past two seasons, in the RCA Dome Sunday at 1 p.m.

"We played pretty good this week, but we've got another big divisional game in Jacksonville," said Colts defensive tackle Raheem Brock, who registered 1.5 of the Colts four sacks.

The victory also gave the Colts a 15-2 record in the RCA Dome over the last two seasons. They have won their last four home openers.

The Colts now are 9-0 against the Texans in Houston's five-year history. The Colts are the only AFC South team the Texans never have beaten.

"Coming up here is a chore," Texans quarterback

Houston Texans at Indianapolis Colts

Score by Quarters	1	2	3	4	Score
Houston Texans	0	3	0	21	24
Indianapolis Colts	14	6	10	13	43

Defensive team captain Gary Brackett made sure the team would not suffer a letdown against Houston, holding the Texans to three points through the first three quarters.

David Carr said.

Colts Head Coach Tony Dungy spoke to the team extensively this week about not looking past the Texans, but said he never particularly worried it would be an issue.

"Our guys like to play and they understand how those things work," Dungy said. "We've had a lot of situations where people talk about how one team has beaten another team (an extended number of times). It's all how you play that day and how you prepare that week.

"I think that's why we've been good. We prepare hard and well. It doesn't really matter who we play."

The Colts were dominant offensively throughout, and defensively for the first three quarters.

Manning completed passes to nine different receivers, finishing with his seventh career 400-yard

Manning completed 26 passes on 38 attempts for three TDs and no picks against the Texans defense.

game. Reggie Wayne and Marvin Harrison each had more than 100-yards receiving, with Harrison passing Art Monk into fifth place on the NFL's all-time receptions list.

Robert Mathis, the team's sacks leader a year ago, had two of the Colts four sacks defensively. The Colts limited the Texans to 105 first-half yards.

"We wanted to cause havoc all day long, and I think for the most part, we did that," Reagor said.

The Colts extended a 20-3 lead by dominating the third quarter. First, Manning passed 15 yards to tight end Bryan Fletcher for a 27-3 lead, and with 3:17 remaining in the third quarter, kicker Adam Vinatieri's third field goal of the game without a miss – a 38-yarder – gave Indianapolis its biggest lead of the game, 30-3.

"We've just been sharp on offense, the whole training camp and all preseason," Dungy said. "We've scored early and gotten up on people. I think it's just maturity on our offense, being sharp. We left some points out there, but we're moving the ball and making things happen."

Houston produced most of its offense in the fourth quarter, scoring three touchdowns and producing 209 yards in the period.

They trimmed the Colts lead several times in the fourth period, but touchdowns runs by Dominic Rhodes (two yards) and Ran Carthon (three yards) – kept the Texans from ever cutting the Colts lead below 20 points.

The passing game, after producing 272 yards against the Giants in the opener, continued to be effective, with Manning working with the a slew of different receivers to give the Colts a seventeen-point halftime lead.

The defense made a huge contribution, too.

On the Texans' first drive, Colts defensive end Robert Mathis sacked David Carr on the first play of the game. Carr fumbled on the ensuing play, and Colts defensive tackle Raheem Brock recovered at the Texans 16.

"You always want to jump out fast and let them know it's going to be a long day," Mathis said.

Three plays later, Manning threw his first touchdown pass of the game, giving the Colts a 7-0 lead with a 10-yard pass to wide receiver Brandon Stokley, who got his feet down just inside the rear corner of the end zone.

After the Texans failed to pick up a first down on their next possession, the Colts drove 63 yards on six plays, with Manning passing 16 yards to rookie running back Joseph Addai for a 14-0 lead. The play was the first NFL touchdown for Addai, the Colts first-round selection in this past April's NFL Draft.

The Colts extended their lead to 17-0 with a 39-yard field goal by Adam Vinatieri midway through the second quarter. After a 43-yard field goal by Kris Brown cut the Colts lead to 14, Vinatieri converted a 43-yard field goal on the half's final play to make it 20-3, Colts.

The Colts had several chances to lead by more at halftime, something that kept Dungy from full celebration afterward. Addai, who rushed for 82 yards 16 carries, fumbled at the goal line in the second quarter, with the Texans recovering in thc cnd zonc for a touchback. And later in the half, a touchdown pass to Reggie Wayne was nullified by a penalty.

Still, a 19-point victory in the division is a victory, onc that scnds the Colts into next week's division game against Jacksonville assured at least of a share of first place.

And one that showed that the Colts can be difficult team to trap.

"We just emphasize playing our game every week," Dungy said. "We have veteran guys who practice hard no matter what the situation. We have a lot of guys who want to play, who don't want to come out of games. They have a lot of pride in their craft. I never worry about our team being up or ready to go. They like to practice and they like to play.

"It was good to get a win in the division and start off at home the way we wanted to. I thought we were a little bit sloppy on a couple of things and that caused us some headaches in the first half. The second half, we really got going until the end when we substituted on defense and really didn't finish up as crisp as we wanted. But we controlled the momentum and controlled the game. I thought we did some awfully good things. We just have to clean up our mistakes a little bit.

"Obviously, another big home division game next week. I think we'll be ready to go." **XLI**

Sunday, September 24, 2006

FIGHTING BACK

Colts Take Sole Possession of First Place with Victory over Jacksonville

Sometimes, statistics matter a great deal.

Often in recent seasons, a glance at the post-game statistics reveals exactly why the Colts won or lost. Sunday was not one of those times. On Sunday, in a crucial early-season AFC South game against the Jacksonville Jaguars, the Colts were out-performed in nearly every "important" statistical category:

• Yards rushing.

• Total yards.

• First downs.

• Time of possession.

The Jacksonville Jaguars, in fact, completely dominated time of possession throughout the match-up of AFC South unbeatens, 39:24-20:46. And yet . . .

Colts 21, Jaguars 14.

The Colts (3-0), playing without several key injured players, overcame a seven-point first-half deficit with touchdowns in the second, third and fourth quarters to take a 14-point lead, holding off the Jaguars (2-1) to take sole possession of first place in the AFC South in front of 57,041 at the RCA Dome Sunday afternoon.

"I take my hat off to the Jaguars," Colts Head Coach Tony Dungy said. "They came in with an excellent plan and they really got the jump on us. After playing a real physical game on Monday night, to travel and come back six days later and play like that, they did a great job. . . .

"I take my hat off to our guys, too. We didn't play our best, but we fought well and we held serve. We'll continue to play better."

The victory was the Colts 11th consecutive victory against AFC South opponents, with the last loss coming in October of 2004 against Jacksonville.

The Colts, who have won the division title each of the last three seasons, have not been out of first place in the AFC South since October of 2004, two weeks after the loss to Jacksonville.

"Whenever you can win a division game, it almost counts twice," said Colts defensive end Dwight Freeney, who played despite a buttock injury that kept him out of practice throughout the week. "It gives you

Jacksonville Jaguars at Indianapolis Colts

Score by Quarters	1	2	3	4	Score
Jacksonville Jaguars	7	0	0	7	14
Indianapolis Colts	0	7	7	7	21

Cornerback Jason David intercepted a pass in the Colts hard-fought 21-14 win against a tough Jacksonville squad.

the advantage, the tiebreaker advantage, and also gives you separation.

"It's a huge game, bigger than any game we've played this year."

The Colts played without Pro Bowl safety Bob Sanders, kicker Adam Vinatieri, wide receiver Brandon Stokley and defensive tackle Corey Simon. The 3-0 start is the third such start in the last four seasons for the Colts. They started 5-0 in 2003 and 13-0 last season.

The Jaguars, the runners-up in the division the last two seasons, have won 10 of their last 12 regular season games, with the only two losses in that span coming against Indianapolis. The Colts - 22-4 in the division since its 2002 inception - have won the last three meetings between the teams, including a sweep last season.

"The better team always gets the victory whether we like it or not," Jaguars running back Fred Taylor said. "We understand what we did and we have to grow from within and this is where it starts.

"We missed a couple of opportunities. We will just go back to the drawing board and get ready for the next team. They deserve all the credit."

Despite the first-half statistical dominance - 185-66 in total yardage and 24:31-5:29 time of possession - the game was tied after two quarters, 7-7.

The Jaguars scored on a 4-yard touchdown run by quarterback Byron Leftwich after an opening possession that used nearly half the first quarter, but Jacksonville didn't score again until 3:32 remaining.

"It was frustrating," said Leftwich, who completed 16 of 28 passes for 107 yards and a touchdown with two interceptions for a 47.8 passer rating. "We have to do a better job at doing something. We have to watch film to really see what happened, but we have do to a better job.

"When you have the ball that much time, you have to come away with more than seven points."

The Jaguars' statistical edges for the game:

- Rushing yards: 191-63.
- Total yards: 297-272.
- First downs: 20-14.

But after an 82-yard punt return for a touchdown by Terrence Wilkins early in the second quarter, statistics notwithstanding, the Colts controlled the game.

The Jaguars rushed for 157 yards on 29 first-half carries, a 5.4-yards-per-carry average. Rookie running back Maurice Jones-Drew led the Jaguars with 87 yards on eight first-half carries, and veteran Fred Taylor added 67 yards on 17 first-half carries.

The Colts held the Jaguars to 22 yards on seven third-quarter carries, and after the first half, the Jaguars had just 34 yards rushing.

"It basically came down to us making hits," Colts linebacker Cato June said. "We just got back to basic tackling in the second half. We did a lot of the same things in the second half. But we came out with an attitude and just wanted to make plays."

Manning, after completing 5 of 13 passes for 63 yards with no touchdowns in the first half, finished 14 of 31 for 219 yards and a touchdown.

Of the Colts 272 total yards, 206 came in the second half.

"We know going into each game with them, they're going to try to run the clock out as much as possible," Colts wide receiver Reggie Wayne said. "You know you're going to have opportunities. You've got to capitalize on them.

"The first half was real slow for us. We came in and made some adjustments."

After Jaguars kicker Josh Scobee knocked a 24-yard field goal off the left upright late in the second quarter, the Colts drove into Jaguars territory, narrowly missing on a chance to take the lead when Colts quarterback Peyton Manning and wide receiver Marvin Harrison barely missed connection at the goal line on a long pass from the Jaguars 40.

The Colts took a lead they never relinquished on the first series of the second half. Taking the second-half kickoff, Indianapolis drove 80 yards on seven plays with Manning capping the drive with a 30-yard touchdown pass to tight end Dallas Clark, who came free on the right side of the field near the goal line.

A 38-yard pass from Manning to Harrison gave the Colts a first down at the Jaguars 31, setting up the go-ahead touchdown.

A 2-yard rollout by Manning midway through the fourth quarter pushed the Colts lead to 14 before a Jaguars' late rally.

"It was something we saw on the sideline," Dungy said. "They were very aggressive pursuing and we thought wc could get it."

Dungy, Manning said, deserved far more credit than that. After seeing the Jaguars' safeties blitz off the edge on 1st-and-goal from the 1 to stop rookie Joseph Addai for a 1-yard loss, Dungy told offensive coordinator Tom Moore to tell Manning to run the naked bootleg.

Manning told no one else, faking to Addai, then pulling the ball back before running alone around the already-committed defense.

"It came from the head coach and once we had clearance on that, I knew we were safe to go," Manning said.

On the possession after Manning's touchdown run, the Jaguars drove 49 yards, with Leftwich throwing seven yards to rookie running back Maurice Jones-Drew to make it 21-14 with 3:32 remaining.

When the Colts managed just one first down on the next series, the Jaguars had a final chance to tie. On 2nd-and-10 from the Jaguars 42, Leftwich threw deep to wide receiver Reggie Williams, but safety Mike Doss cut in front of the pass for the game-securing interception.

"We continue to fight," Freeney said. "We did a great job of hanging in there."

Dungy and several Colts players said as important a sequence came in the middle two quarters, when the Colts moved ahead despite two controversial plays, both of which went against Indianapolis.

On the drive after Scobee's attempt hit the upright, two calls went against the Colts. First, an apparent 51-yard pass from Manning to Colts wide receiver Reggie Wayne was reversed after review. Wayne said he was surprised at the reversal, while Dungy said he wasn't.

Later on the drive, Manning threw deep to Harrison near the goal line. Harrison barely missed the pass, and although Jaguars cornerback Rashean Mathis touched the back of Harrison's shoulder pads, no interference call was made.

The teams left the field to the sounds of the RCA Dome crowd booing the officials, and on the first drive of the second half, Manning found Clark to give the Colts a lead.

Jacksonville never again seriously challenged for the lead.

"It was a tough day," Dungy said. "They were playing very hard, playing well. We were just off a little bit. I thought our sideline stayed calm. We made some adjustments. We did keep our composure. . . .

"This was a good game with two really good teams. We know we'll see these guys again. They'll be chasing us the rest of the way. Hopefully, we can stay in front of him, but it will be fun. They've got a real, real good ball club."

Said Manning, "Obviously, you have to move on. At the time, if you spend a lot of time complaining about it, it's going to affect you the next play. After that play to Reggie, everybody was disappointed, but we came back and got a third-down conversion.

"I thought we should have gotten some points on that possession, but you have to stay poised and offensively, we have been in enough games and guys have been around enough to know it's going to be a four-quarter game and you have to move on from there." **XLI**

Sunday, October 1, 2006

DRAMA IN NEW JERSEY

Manning Rallies Indianapolis Twice in Meadowlands

All that was needed was a drive for the ages.

The Colts needed a touchdown, not a field goal.

They had no timeouts. And to cap the whole situation off, it had to be done in the nation's biggest media market – in front of a hostile crowd on a day when things hadn't exactly gone the Colts way.

So, what did Peyton Manning and the offense do?

They came through.

Not once, but twice.

Manning, a six-time Pro Bowl quarterback and a two-time Most Valuable Player, drove the Colts to two touchdowns in the final 2:32, twice rallying the Colts from four-point deficits in a 31-28 victory over the New York Jets in front of 77,190 at the New Jersey Meadowlands Sunday afternoon.

"It was a great win, obviously," said Manning, who completed 11 of 14 passes on the final two drives for 96 yards and a touchdown, also running for a 1-yard sneak with 50 seconds remaining that provided the final margin.

"I think tomorrow we'll start analyzing, going back at the things we could have done early. But right now, these are the ones you want to try to enjoy. (Colts Head) Coach (Tony) Dungy kind of reminded us afterward: We do know how to win games and close games."

On Sunday, Manning saved the best for last, and had to come through twice.

With 2:24 remaining, Manning capped a 12-play, 68-yard drive with a 2-yard, blitz-beating touchdown pass to reserve tight end Bryan Fletcher.

Colts 24, Jets 21.

"You can't quit," Colts wide receiver Reggie Wayne said. "We did too much in the off-season to quit. We always talk about playing 60 minutes, and that's what we did today."

The Colts offense retreated to the bench, but before most players could sit, Jets kick returner Justin Miller set a team record with a 103-yard kickoff return to give the Jets a 28-24 lead with 2:20 remaining.

Terrence Wilkins returned to the ensuing kickoff to the Colts 39.

Nine plays and 1:30 later, one play after Manning

Indianapolis Colts at New York Jets

Score by Quarters	1	2	3	4	Score
Indianapolis Colts	7	7	0	17	31
New York Jets	0	14	0	14	28

A stubborn Jets team fought the high-flying Colts and had the lead in the fourth quarter until the Colts prevailed.

passed 15 yards to wide receiver Reggie Wayne on 2nd-and-10 from the 16, Manning snuck the ball over from the 1.

Colts 31, Jets 24.

"There truly was never any panic," Manning said. "When they ran the kickoff back, we didn't really have time to get mad or panic. (Colts offensive linemen) Jeff (Saturday) and Tarik (Glenn) were just kind of getting to the bench and sitting down and all of a sudden, you see that guy scoring."

Manning had just gotten on the telephone to speak with assistant head coach/quarterbacks Jim Caldwell.

"I had to hang up with him," Manning said with a laugh.

Each week in practice, the Colts work on the situation: 1:30-to-1:40 remaining with no timeouts. On Sunday, it was for real.

"It just all came together," Colts offensive guard Dylan Gandy said. "I think the key is what coach talked about: everybody on our team believed that we were going to go score. There wasn't a doubt.

"It was definitely emotionally not great, but at the same time, we've got a job to do. We're confident in our preparation and in our ability to execute what we're coached to do."

And after Manning's touchdown run, the lead held. After a last-play, five-lateral, three-fumble desperation play by the Jets ended with Colts cornerback Jason David recovering a fumble, the Colts had secured a 4-0 start for the third time in four seasons.

"We're very fortunate," Dungy said. "I don't want to take anything away from our offense – they made two drives when we had to. That's what we expect. We've got a very group and we wouldn't expect anything less, but to put ourselves in that situation wasn't good."

Added Dungy, "We just weren't sharp. We've got to be

Defensive leader Montae Reagor produced a sack to help energize the Colts defense.

better. We will be."

The victory came in a match-up of AFC division leaders, with the victory maintaining Indianapolis' sole possession of first place in the AFC South. The Jets entered the game with a share of the lead in the AFC East.

"I told our team in the locker room, 'We're obviously very fortunate to win,'" Dungy said. "The one good thing I do like about our team is we know how to win and we play hard for 60 minutes and we seem to find a way to win these games.

"I have to take my hat off to the New York Jets, and their staff. They've done a great job. They play to win. They did what you need to do to slow us down.

"It was one of those games that could have gone either way."

Of the offense's fourth-quarter performance, Dungy said, "We expect that. We practice that all the time. We practice 1:30, no timeouts, so it didn't surprise anybody in our locker room we were able to do that. You shouldn't have to do it twice in a game.

"It wasn't a surprise. We've seen it so much we kind of expect it."

Time and time again on the final two drives, Manning and the offense made clutch plays. Among the biggest came on 3rd-and-6 from the Jets 35 with the Colts trailing 28-24 with 1:26 remaining. Working from the shotgun, Manning was pressured. He started to run, then made an off-balance throw to Marvin Harrison for a 19-yard gain.

"Marvin probably would have scored if I hadn't thrown him out of bounds," Manning said. "That was a huge third-down conversion."

That play came in the wake of Miller's return, something Manning said didn't discourage the Colts offense.

"It can be deflating if it's the last play of the game," Manning said. "When you know you have time to go out there and do something about it, you don't sit there and talk about it. You just talk about what you're going to do right now. There wasn't a whole lot of talk by the offensive line. The offense just said, 'Hey, here are the plays we're thinking. Let's go down and get it in the end zone.'"

The completion to Harrison came four plays before Manning's one-yard sneak, after which Manning spiked the ball in the end zone.

"I was pumped," Manning said. "You practice those two-minute drills all the time in practice. Everybody's played that backyard game where you envision yourself: last play of the game, last drive – what are you going to do? Anytime you can do it in New York, it adds a little something to it."

The Colts took momentum early in the half, then entered halftime tied at 14-14 despite struggling at times offensively.

On the Jets' first drive, Colts defensive end Robert Mathis got around Jets offensive tackle D'Brickashaw Ferguson – the fourth overall selection in last April's NFL Draft – and sacked Chad Pennington for an eight-yard loss. Mathis forced Pennington to fumble and Colts defensive end Josh Thomas recovered.

Six plays later, Colts running back Dominic Rhodes' six-yard run gave Indianapolis a 7-0 lead with 12:28 remaining in the first quarter.

The Jets held thc Colts to two first downs over the next 23 minutes, and with 9:10 remaining bcforc halftime, they tied the game when Pennington threw deep over the middle to wide receiver Jerricho Cotchery, who turned a 20-yard pass into a 33-yard catch and run touchdown.

After a successful onside kick, the Jets drove 57 yards on 11 plays, taking a 14-7 lead when running back Kevan Barlow rushed for a 1-yard touchdown.

That touchdown was set up by a pass interference call against Colts safety Antoine Bethea, who knocked away a pass at the goal line intended for Cotchery. The call gave New York a 1st-and-goal at the Indianapolis 1.

On the first play of the ensuing series, Manning threw deep to Colts wide receiver Reggie Wayne, whose 41-yard reception gave the Colts a first down at the Jets 44.

Ten plays later, Colts rookie running back Joseph Addai's 2-yard run made it 14-14 with 16 seconds remaining in the half. The teams were then scoreless in the third quarter before a dramatic, 31-point fourth quarter.

"We've got some veteran players who know how to make big plays at crunch time," Dungy said. "We certainly couldn't seem to do much of anything right. We had a lot of things happen that could cost you a game and will cost you a game if we're not careful. The big thing is we came away with a victory.

"We'll learn from it and go from there." **XLI**

Sunday, October 8, 2006

STILL UNBEATEN

Colts Rally for a 14-13 Victory over Tennessee to Remain Unbeaten

Really, only a few statistics mattered Sunday afternoon.

Actually, make that one statistic. The AFC South-leading Colts made it to the bye week unbeaten Sunday, doing so with a rally in the fourth quarter for the second consecutive week, beating the winless Tennessee Titans, 14-13, in front of 57,021 at the RCA Dome.

Players afterward weren't thrilled.

They spoke mostly of needing to improve, and of just how they can make certain areas better. But they spoke of something else, too:

How, after five weeks of the NFL season, they are unbeaten.

That, players and coaches said, is special.

No matter how they got there.

"Five-and-oh is 5-0 – a win is a win," Colts wide receiver Reggie Wayne said.

"We didn't play maybe as well as we can play," Colts Head Coach Tony Dungy said. "But our guys again in the second half did what we had to do to win. So, that's the good news – we are 5-0 and probably the next good news is that we've got a bye coming up.

"We are not playing as well as we need to play. It's probably my job to get us better."

The Colts (5-0), unbeaten after five games for the third time in four seasons, maintained their two-game lead in the AFC South with the victory. They are idle next week, after which Indianapolis will play host to Washington (2-3).

The Colts, who trailed throughout the game, took their first lead with 5:10 remaining, allowed 214 yards rushing, the third game this season in which the Colts have allowed more than 180 yards rushing.

"We're 5-0," Colts Pro Bowl linebacker Cato June said. "We're not really worried about, 'This game, that game.' We're 5-0. Whether we give up 500 yards rushing, if we win, you can't really be mad at that. . . ."

Colts quarterback Peyton Manning, held to 56 first-half passing yards, threw second-half touchdown passes to wide receivers Marvin Harrison (third quarter) and Reggie Wayne (fourth quarter).

Tennessee Titans at Indianapolis Colts

Score by Quarters	1	2	3	4	Score
Tennessee Titans	7	3	3	0	13
Indianapolis Colts	0	0	7	7	14

The Colts had to scramble for a victory against a Titans team that got stronger as the season went along.

"Every time you play a game, you're prepared for a fourth-quarter, down-to-the-wire, last-minute-drive game," Manning said. "That's how you always prepare for AFC South games. We were fortunate to make enough plays to win today.

"There's not a lot of trickery. It really comes down to execution."

The Jacksonville Jaguars, the second-place team in the AFC South, stayed within two games of Indianapolis with a victory in Jacksonville over the New York Jets. The victory extended the Colts AFC South winning streak to 12 games.

The Colts, who have a 3-0 record in the South this season, haven't lost a division game since October 2004.

They have won seven consecutive games against Tennessee, which lost to Dallas, 45-14, last week.

"You can't take any game lightly," Colts middle linebacker Gary Brackett said. "It's tough, but guys are going to try to win and that's what they tried to today."

Said wide receiver Brandon Stokley, "Hats off to them. They played a great game and executed well."

The Colts last season won a third consecutive AFC South title and did so in dominating fashion. They won their first 13 games of the season, rarely trailing in the fourth quarter and winning all 13 games by seven or more points.

That was an NFL record for consecutive victories by

In his first game back following an injury in Week Two, Brandon Stokley provided a lift and led Colts receivers with five receptions for 57 yards against Tennessee.

a touchdown or more.

This season has been a different story, with four of the Colts victories coming by seven points or less. Wayne, afterward, spoke of the Colts finding a new identity this season, an identity that includes winning closer games than in previous year, and Dungy said he wasn't concerned about the recent trend of late rallies.

"I don't worry about that at all," Dungy said. "We've won some games this year in different ways. We didn't have to win them this way last year. I think this is going to hold us in good stead. Really, these are more like games you're going to play.

"There are going to be games you've got to win in the fourth quarter and there are going to be tight situations when things don't always go well. Last year was one of those unbelievable runs that we were on. I don't think you can compare things to last year.

"Last year, we did a lot of things right. Those aren't going to come along as often as you'd like them to. This is more what the NFL is all about and we've managed to win five of these games this way."

And in each of the last three victories – over Jacksonville in the RCA Dome in Week 3, last week in

Mike Doss had an interception and led a Colts secondary that limited Tennessee to 63 passing yards.

the Meadowlands against the Jets and Sunday against the Titans – they have trailed before rallying. Last week, the Colts twice overcame four-point fourth-quarter deficits with late fourth-quarter touchdown drives.

"We can't really rely on that," Dungy said. "We can't fall back on that. We have to play better all the way across the board and I think we will."

On Sunday, it wasn't quite as dramatic as a week before.

But still, late-game heroics were needed.

The Colts, who trailed 7-0 after the first quarter, 10-0 at halftime and 13-7 after the third quarter, still trailed by six points with 9:38 remaining after rookie T.J. Rushing returned a punt eight yards to the Titans 43.

Manning, whose red-zone interception off the hands of Wayne ended the Colts previous drive at the Titans 4, threw again to Wayne on 3rd-and-8 from the Titans 41. On a play that Manning later called one of the game's crucial moments, Wayne made a diving reception for 1st-and-10 at the Titans 29.

Seven plays later, on 3rd-and-goal from the 2, Manning again threw to Wayne.

This time, Wayne caught the pass just over the goal line before being pushed out of the end zone. Martin Gramatica's point after gave the Colts a 14-13 lead with 5:10 remaining.

"I just think, more than anything, we're a team that's

going to find a way to win," June said. "We put ourselves in a hole. I don't know if we enjoy that or something. Every week, we seem to find a way to put ourselves in a hole then battle out."

The Colts relied on a familiar combination to cut into the Titans' halftime lead. With 6:16 remaining in the third quarter, Manning passed 13 yards to Marvin Harrison, the seven-time Pro Bowl wide receiver. The play went for a touchdown and cut the Titans' lead to 10-7.

"The main difference was our execution improved in the second half," Manning said.

Before Sunday, Wayne and Harrison hadn't caught a touchdown pass in four games this season.

"We came in at halftime and nobody panicked," Wayne said. "Nobody was blaming anybody. We came in, made some corrections and got going in the second half."

With the Titans leading by a touchdown, Manning threw short to running back Dominic Rhodes on 3rd-and-8 from the Colts 45. Rhodes fumbled and Titans linebacker Keith Bulluck recovered at the Colts 49.

The Titans then drove 45 yards on seven plays to take a 10-0 lead on a 22-yard field goal by Rob Bironas.

At halftime, the Titans had rushed for 152 yards and a touchdown on 21 first-half carries, a 7.2-yards-per-carry average. Titans quarterback Vince Young's 19-yard touchdown run gave Tennessee a 7-0 lead with 6:41 remaining in the first quarter.

Manning finished the first half 9 of 17 passing for 56 yards and no touchdowns with no interceptions.

The difference early was that the Titans finished their first drive and the Colts narrowly missed on theirs. The result was a 7-0 Titans lead after a quarter.

The Colts took the opening kickoff and drove efficiently into Titans territory. On 3rd-and-6 from the Titans 37, Manning threw deep to Wayne. The pass was inches over his reach.

On the ensuing series, the Titans drove 88 yards on seven plays, moving effectively on the ground. Young capped the drive with a 19-yard run to give the Titans an early lead they wouldn't relinquish until late in a game closer than many expected.

"It was close, but we got the cigar." **XLI**

Sunday, October 22, 2006

GUTS AND GLORY

Bloodied in First Half, Manning Leads Colts to Victory in Second

In eight NFL seasons, Peyton Manning has made the memorable performance commonplace. On Sunday, he turned in another.

One that shouldn't be easily forgotten.

Manning, bloodied, battered and beaten up late in the first half, had some in the sold-out RCA Dome crowd of 57,724 wondering at halftime if he would play in the third quarter, not running from the tunnel for the second half until seconds before kickoff.

Play he did. Memorably so.

Manning, a two-time Most Valuable Player in his ninth season as the Colts quarterback, played a near-perfect third quarter, turning a one-point halftime deficit into a commanding Indianapolis lead. He threw three third-quarter touchdown passes – two to wide receiver Marvin Harrison – and the Colts beat the Washington Redskins, 36-22, at the RCA Dome Sunday afternoon.

"He's a little tougher than people give him credit for," Colts Head Coach Tony Dungy said after Manning's three-touchdown third-quarter keyed a day on which he completed 25 of 35 passes for 342 yards and four touchdowns with no interceptions for a season-high 140.4 passer rating.

Dungy added, "He said he was ready to go. At halftime, I asked him if he was OK. He said he was fine and back to normal. He was on fire in the third quarter. . . .

"We never like to see our quarterback get hit. He got hit a couple of times today. Fortunately, he got through it."

How hot was Manning's quarter?

Consider:

First drive: Two passes, two completions, 25 yards. It ended with a 4-yard touchdown pass to in Harrison for a 20-14 Colts lead.

Second drive: Two passes, two completions, 60 yards. It ended with a 51-yard touchdown pass to wide receiver Reggie Wayne for a 27-14 Colts lead.

Third drive: Four passes, three completions, 53 yards. It ended with a 1-yard touchdown pass to Harrison for a 33-14 Colts lead.

"I'm always looking for Marvin and Reggie," Manning

Washington Redskins at Indianapolis Colts

Score by Quarters	1	2	3	4	Score
Washington Redskins	0	14	0	8	22
Indianapolis Colts	7	6	20	3	36

After giving up 14 second-quarter points, defensive tackle Darrell Reid and his teammates clamped down and held the Redskins to eight points in the fourth quarter.

said. "They had different guys covering them and when it's true one-on-one, it's hard to cover those guys. We finally got them into some man-to-man looks. They were playing quite a bit of zone early, and we finally caught them in some man-to-man looks and we able to hut some big plays on them.

"When you have Reggie Wayne and Marvin Harrison out there, you can't ask for a better scenario."

The third-quarter performance came after Manning was hit hard several times in the second quarter, including one play on which he was hit hard enough that he called a time-out after the play.

"I don't spend a lot of time thinking or talking about it," Manning said. "Nobody likes to burn a timeout. I'd rather take a delay-of-game penalty sometimes than call a first- or second-quarter timeout.

"For me to call a timeout right there meant I needed another minute to get it together right there."

After a 14-13 halftime deficit, Peyton Manning had three third-quarter touchdown passes, leading the Colts to a 36-22 victory over Washington. Manning had a seasonal-best four touchdown passes to go along with 342 passing yards.

Manning downplayed the injury aspect of his performance, declining to discuss specifics and smiling when several reporters pushed the issue.

"You're not going to get much from me on that," Manning said.

The victory gave the Colts a 6-0 record for the second consecutive season, and moved them three games ahead of Jacksonville in the AFC South. The Jaguars lost at Houston on Sunday, 27-7.

With the victory, the Colts became the ninth team in NFL history to start two consecutive seasons with a record of 6-0. The others: Buffalo (1920-21), Green Bay (1929-31), Chicago (1933-34), Dallas (1968-69), Los Angeles (1968-69), Chicago (1985-86), Denver (1997-98) and St. Louis (1999-2001).

The Colts visit the AFC West-leading Denver Broncos Sunday, then will visit AFC East-leading New England the following Sunday.

"We're proud of our guys," Dungy said. "We'll enjoy this one this week and start focusing on Denver."

Defensively, the Colts – after entering the game ranked

32nd in the NFL against the run – allowed the Redskins 114 yards rushing, more than 50 yards below their season average. They also held the Redskins to one offensive touchdown in the first 59 minutes.

"The guys went out there and played with a little swagger and we moved to the ball," Colts linebacker Gary Brackett said.

The game was the 14th of Manning's career with four or more touchdown passes. The NFL record is 21, held by former Miami Dolphins quarterback Dan Marino.

Manning left the field at halftime several seconds before the rest of the team and didn't return from the locker room until seconds before the start of the second half. The dramatic entrance was a prelude to memorable third quarter.

Manning, the Colts two-time National Football League Most Valuable Players, threw three third-quarter touchdown passes, turning a one-point halftime deficit into a 33-14 lead entering the fourth quarter.

Harrison's touchdown receptions were the 112th and 113th of his career. He is now tied with running back Lenny Moore for first-place on the team's all-time touchdowns list.

The Colts outgained the Redskins 202-55 in the quarter. So efficient were the Colts that they faced just one third down in the period.

It wasn't all passing for the Colts, either. Rookie running back Joseph Addai, the team's first-round selection in last April's NFL Draft, rushed seven times for 64 yards in the period, making key plays on all three scoring drives.

Addai finished with a career-high 85 yards on 11 carries, a 7.1-yards-per-carry average.

The Colts, who had played from behind in their most recent three games, took a step early to prevent that. They stopped the Redskins on three downs on the game's first possession, then moved quickly to take a 7-0 lead in front of a jam-packed crowd at the RCA Dome.

The Colts drove 92 yards on 11 plays, with Manning passing one yard to tight end Dallas Clark. Three plays earlier, Manning set up the touchdown with a 40-yard pass to Clark on a play-action play.

The Redskins managed three first downs in the quarter. The Colts had possession in the quarter once more, but did not pick up a first down.

Late in the second quarter, a huge punt return cost them the lead. With the Colts holding a 10-7 lead, Washington Redskins wide receiver Antwaan Randle El – who played collegiately at Indiana University – returned a punt 87 yards for a second-quarter touchdown that gave the Redskins their only lead.

Manning led Indianapolis on a 52-yard drive late in the second quarter to pull the Colts to within one, 14-13. Adam Vinatieri kicked a 19-yard field goal with eight seconds remaining before halftime.

"We were just a little out of sync in the first half," Dungy said. "In the second half, we got organized at halftime and we very sharp."

That the Colts got better after halftime didn't surprise Dungy. He said he worried all week about starting slowly, particularly after the team's off week last weekend. A 23-point second half, one in which the Colts pulled away from a team that made the playoffs last season and entered Sunday's game calling it a must-win, was a positive sign, Dungy said.

"It was a good win for us, and I think something we can build on," Dungy said, adding, "I thought we played a little better, more our style, in the third quarter. We got more into it. I was concerned about the slow start.

"But I think we're getting better. I saw signs of it during the bye week and this week in practice. Hopefully, we'll continue to make progress." **XLI**

Sunday, October 29, 2006

MILE-HIGH DRAMA

Colts Rally Past AFC West-Leading Denver for 34-31 Victory

The questions came over and over.

They came from different angles after the Colts 34-31 victory over the Denver Broncos in front of 76,767 at INVESCO Field at Mile High late Sunday afternoon, but all focused on the same topic:

Just how good was Peyton Manning's performance?

Was Colts Head Coach Tony Dungy surprised?

Or struck by it in any particular way?

Dungy, speaking in the wake of a dramatic, come-from-behind victory that maintained the Colts status as the AFC's last remaining unbeaten team, fielded a few of the questions, saying at first that it was what the Colts pretty much expected from Manning.

Then answered as succinctly as possible.

"You can't overemphasize how good the quarterback is," Dungy said.

That has been true around the Colts (7-0) throughout the career of Manning – the Colts six-time Pro Bowl quarterback – and it was true again against the AFC West-leading Denver Broncos (5-2) Sunday.

Playing against the NFL's fourth-ranked defense, a unit that had allowed two touchdowns in the first six games of the season – a feat not achieved in the NFL since 1934 – Manning proved again why he is considered one of the league's elite players.

Manning, the National Football League's Most Valuable Player in 2003 and 2004 and the runner-up for the award last season, completed 32 of 39 passes for 345 yards and three touchdowns, all of which went to wide receiver Reggie Wayne.

And all came in the second half.

It was a second half the Colts entered trailing 14-6, and one in which the Colts – the NFL's third-ranked offense entering the game – scored on each of their five possessions, a half entering which Manning said the Colts discussed finishing drives and "playing perfect."

"That's what they make you do – they make you execute," Manning said. "We talked about really concentrating on one-play-at-a-time, because we moved the ball well in the first half, but they tightened up down there and made more plays in the red zone than we did.

"The second half, it was the other way around."

Indianapolis Colts at Denver Broncos

Score by Quarters	1	2	3	4	Score
Indianapolis Colts	3	3	14	14	34
Denver Broncos	0	14	7	10	31

Reggie Wayne had 10 catches for 138 yards and tied a club record with three touchdown receptions at Denver. Wayne also added a two-point conversion in the comeback win.

Wayne caught 10 passes for 138 yards and three touchdowns, helping the Colts overcome a defensive performance that Dungy said later pleased few players.

The Broncos produced 396 total yards, rushing for 227 yards on 36 carries and scoring on their final three possessions.

"You know they (the Broncos) have an excellent defense, and you know they run the ball well," Manning said. "We just tried to be efficient in our possessions. We didn't think there would be many possessions. I think we had three in the first half and I don't know how many we had in the second half. We were just trying to be efficient."

How close to perfection were the Colts offensively in the second half?

Four times in the second half the Colts took possession trailing by less than a touchdown or tied. On all four possessions, the Colts took the lead on the possession.

The final time? That came on the final series of the game, when the Colts took possession at their 20 with the game tied, 31-31.

"When our offense has the ball with a chance to win, we feel pretty good about it no matter who we're playing," Dungy said.

Eight plays later, Colts kicker Adam Vinatieri's 37-yard field goal – his fourth of the game without a miss – gave the Colts the winning points with two seconds remaining.

On the drive, Manning completed five of five passes for 47 yards.

For the fourth quarter, Manning completed 14 of 16 passes for 164 yards and a touchdown, a performance that came against a secondary that Manning said includes two of the league's top cover corners – perennial Pro Bowl selection Champ Bailey and Darrent Williams.

"That is why you work in April, May and June," Manning said. "That's why you throw routes in the off-season with nobody covering. You pretend it's Champ Bailey covering and you have to make a perfect throw, a perfect route. That's why you work out.

"We ran some great routes. Nothing's easy when

you're completing passes against those guys.

"We had some great routes, and of course, the protection was good."

And throughout the second half, the performance of Manning and the Colts offense took on a memorable tone. The game went back and forth, and after Manning's third touchdown pass – a 19-yarder to Reggie Wayne – he celebrated particularly enthusiastically.

"I'm enjoying it," he said with a smile. "You take a hit like I did last week (against the Washington Redskins), it sort of reinforces your priorities. You see the quarterbacks going down like flies (around the rest of the NFL). You kind of enjoy it while you're out there. Don't ever take it for granted."

Despite the emotion, Dungy said, "I thought Peyton was very patient today" and he added, "We're running the same plays we've been running for seven years. He just knows where to go with the ball."

The victory made the Colts the second team in NFL history to start back-to-back seasons with seven consecutive victories. They started 13-0 en route to a third consecutive AFC South title last season.

"We just find a way to win," Colts linebacker Cato June said. "We know how to win in tough situations and tough environments. Denver is going to play is tough. They're a great team. They weren't 5-1 for nothing.

The victory also allowed the Colts to maintain a three-game lead over Jacksonville (4-3) in the AFC South, and moved them two games ahead of every team in the AFC except New England (5-1), which visits Minnesota Monday.

The Colts visit New England Sunday night.

"We hadn't really looked at that," Dungy said. "I think you can get way ahead of yourself. I told the team in there (the locker room), 'We're only in October. We've got to continue to get better.' If we keep improving, we'll be where we'd like to be. But if we think it's this week and next week, then the season's over, that's not going to be the case.

"We've got to improve our run defense, and we've

got to continue to get better. We know we're three games ahead of Jacksonville in our division, and that's all we know right now."

The Colts, who trailed 14-6 at halftime, scored touchdowns on their first two drives of the third quarter – touchdown passes from Manning to Wayne – but the Broncos scored on the final play of the quarter to lead, 21-20.

After stopping the Broncos on the first series of the third quarter, the Colts drove 56 yards on six plays, pulling to within six when Manning passed 12 yards to Wayne with 12:04 remaining in the quarter.

"We were just finishing drives," Wayne said. "We didn't finish drives in the first half. We were settling for field goals."

On the next series, Colts defensive end Raheem Brock recovered a fumble by Broncos quarterback Jake Plummer at the Denver 12. Three plays later, Manning passed five yards to Wayne to give the Colts the lead.

One possession later, the Broncos took a 21-20 lead when running back Mike Bell capped a 14-play drive with a 1-yard run on the quarter's final play.

The Broncos had taken an eight-point halftime lead with a 1-yard touchdown run by quarterback Jake Plummer and a 15-yard touchdown pass from Plummer to wide receiver Javon Walker. Vinatieri made field goals of 42 and 30 yards in the first half, then converted from

The Colts offense scored on each of its five second-half possessions to fuel a 34-31 comeback victory at Denver.

48 yards on the first drive of the fourth quarter to make it, 23-21, Colts.

Denver retook the lead, 28-23, with a 1-yard run by Bell with 8:54 remaining to cap a eight-play, 80-yard drive, but Manning threw 19 yards to Wayne with 3:25 remaining to give the Colts a 29-28 lead.

Manning then passed to Wayne for the two-point conversion and a 31-28 lead.

On the Broncos' ensuing drive, Mike Bell ran for 48 yards on the first play, but the Colts held after that, and Broncos kicker Jason Elam's 49-yard field goal tied it, 31-31.

"When we held them to a field goal, we thought that's what was important," Dungy said.

Because it came with 1:49 remaining, it also gave the Colts and Manning time to drive for a field goal. One of the last things Dungy told Manning before the drive was there was more than enough time remaining, and that the Colts didn't really need to drive too far to get into field-goal range for Vinatieri.

Five passes by Manning later – and two runs for 15 yards by rookie running back Joseph Addai (17 carries, 93 yards) – Vinatieri was lining up for the game-winning kick of one of the season's most memorable games. **XLI**

Sunday, November 5, 2006

STREAKING IN NEW ENGLAND

Colts Beat New England in Foxboro, Mass., for Second Consecutive Season

It wasn't easy.

Then again, it really wasn't supposed to be.

Not against a team that had won three of the past five Super Bowls. Not against a team many consider the Colts nemesis. Not in one of the NFL's toughest venues.

Not with the best record in the AFC at the season's midway point at stake.

Easy or not, the result was the same:

The Colts have a winning streak in Foxboro, Mass.

Yes, that Foxboro, Mass.

With quarterback Peyton Manning passing for more than 300 yards for a team-record tying third consecutive game, and with a maligned defense making clutch plays at important times, the Colts beat the New England Patriots, 27-20, on a cold, clear Sunday night in front of 68,756 at Gillette Stadium.

"It was a great win, a great team win," Manning said after he completed 20 of 36 passes for 326 yards and two touchdowns with an interception for a passer rating of 93.1.

"To beat these guys, especially here, that's got to be as a team. Everybody has to contribute – all phases of it."

All three phases contributed for the Colts Sunday night.

Very notably, the defense contributed in a big way.

Because as much as the victory was about Manning and the Colts offense, and as much as it was about another huge game for Colts wide receiver Marvin Harrison, it was about a Colts defense that had been criticized throughout the season shutting down a Patriots offense that scored 31 points in a nationally-televised victory over Minnesota last week.

On Sunday, the Patriots moved at times, but the most notable statistic was one Colts Head Coach Tony Dungy considers one of the most important:

Turnovers.

As in, five turnovers committed by the normally mistake-free Patriots.

The Colts intercepted Patriots quarterback Tom Brady four times – twice in each half – and the Colts also recovered a Patriots fumble.

Indianapolis Colts at New England Patriots

Score by Quarters	1	2	3	4	Score
Indianapolis Colts	7	10	7	3	27
New England Patriots	0	14	3	3	20

Antoine Bethea made an acrobatic interception as the Colts picked-off Tom Brady four times and beat the Patriots 27-20 in New England.

Marvin Harrison stretches for the catch at New England for one of his two touchdown receptions. Harrison had eight catches for 145 yards.

"It's all about people stepping up," said Colts defensive end Dwight Freeney, who helped pressure Brady into 20-of-35 passing for 201 yards and no touchdowns with the four interceptions for a passer rating of 34.0.

"Defensively, creating those turnovers was absolutely huge," Manning said. "People have been on our defense a little bit. Those guys stepped up and answered."

Said Dungy, "We're finding different ways to win. Tonight, it was the defense and the takeaways."

The victory allowed the Colts (8-0) to maintain their three-game lead in the AFC South, and also gave them the AFC's best record by two games at the season's midway point. The Patriots, Denver Broncos, Baltimore Ravens and San Diego Chargers are all 6-2.

It also was the Colts second consecutive victory in Foxboro.

"We continue to do what we do – we're not worried about past history," Freeney said.

"It was just another game, man," said Colts wide receiver Reggie Wayne, who finished with six receptions for 90 yards. "One thing about this team: we don't fall into all of that, what the critics say about getting over the hump, not being able to win in Foxboro.

"As long as we play our game, like we did tonight, we'll find a way to win."

The victory gave the Colts two road victories in as many weeks over AFC division leaders. The Colts beat Denver, 34-31, in Denver last week.

"It's really not that big of a deal," Dungy said. "Our guys know we're just in the first half of the year. It's Week 8, and win or lose, it wasn't going to determine a lot. We went through this last year, and it's really about getting better.

"That's what our team will try to do, is continue to improve. It's one game."

The Colts, until last season, had lost nine consecutive games to the Patriots in Foxboro, and six consecutive games to the Patriots overall.

"I don't think last year had too much bearing," Dungy said.

It also made the Colts the NFL's last remaining unbeaten team. The Chicago Bears, the NFL's other remaining unbeaten team entering the weekend, lost to the Miami Dolphins, 31-13, in Chicago Sunday.

"We went through it last year and that helps," Dungy said. "Our guys know that it's really not about unbeaten seasons. Right now, we're three games up on Jacksonville (in the AFC South), which is good. We're two games up on everybody in the AFC and we just have to keep playing.

"(Bears Head Coach) Lovie (Smith) let me down today. I was hoping they'd continue to win so they could get all that focus, but we're happy going through the first half like this – going to Denver, to New England, to New York twice, playing Jacksonville at home . . .

"It was a rough stretch and I don't think we could have predicted being 8-0, but we're happy with it."

The victory was the Colts 30th in their last 33 regular season games. They have won 29 consecutive games in which their playoff seeding was undecided.

The Colts, unlike many past games in Foxboro, took an early lead. They scored a touchdown on the game's first possession when Manning passed four yards to wide receiver Marvin Harrison, then scored on all three of their first-half possessions en route to a 17-14 halftime lead.

Colts vs Patriots

Harrison, a seven-time Pro Bowl selection, caught eight passes for 145 yards and two touchdowns, including a spectacular, sideline-defying touchdown in the third quarter that helped the Colts maintain momentum in the second half.

The Patriots, through much of the first half, matched the Colts score for score. After Harrison's touchdown, the Patriots tied it at 7-7 with a 1-yard touchdown run by running back Corey Dillon.

The Colts moved 82 yards on eight plays on the ensuing possession, taking a 14-7 lead when rookie running back Joseph Addai (43 yards, 18 carries) scored on a 1-yard touchdown run with 9:56 remaining. The Patriots then tied it again, 14-14, when Dillon rushed over from four yards with 4:14 remaining in the half.

A 23-yard field goal by Adam Vinatieri – who signed as an unrestricted free agent from the Patriots this past off-season – gave the Colts a 17-14 halftime lead Indianapolis never relinquished.

Safety Bob Sanders intercepted Brady at the Colts 3 with 17 seconds remaining in the half, the Colts second interception of the game. Rookie safety Antoine Bethea intercepted Brady in the end zone to end the Patriots' first drive.

Harrison's tightroping touchdown – he tipped the ball to himself and grazed both feet on the Gillette Stadium turf on the play – pushed the Colts lead to 24-14, and the rest of the game was about maintaining the lead and getting out of Foxboro with a two-game conference lead.

Vinatieri, who missed a 37-yard field goal on the first drive of the second half, made a 31-yarder with 10:17 remaining to push the Colts lead to 27-17.

After a Patriots field goal, the Colts had a chance to all-but clinch the victory with two minutes remaining, but Vinatieri's 46-yard field goal sailed wide right, leaving New England with a final chance to tie.

Brady's first pass on the ensuing drive was a hard, lining pass to tight end Benjamin Watson for a 25-yard gain, but his next pass caromed off the hands of running back Kevin Faulk and linebacker Cato June made his second interception of the game, the team's fourth.

"Really, you just want to be able to measure yourself against the best teams in the AFC – and obviously they are one," Colts center Jeff Saturday said.

"The thing I like about our team is we're finding a way to win," Colts Head Coach Tony Dungy said. "We're still not playing our best, and aren't playing exceptionally sharp all the way around, but we're finding ways to win.

"I'm proud of our guys, because we didn't necessarily keep our poise and we did some things that were uncharacteristic tonight, but we still won.

"We're 8-0, so I guess that's a good sign."

The 8-0 record made for an eerie sense of déjà vu Monday. The Colts left Gillette Stadium 8-0 last season en route to a franchise-best 13-0 start. And while Dungy said this year's team perhaps isn't playing as well two months into the season as last year's, he said he is somehow more pleased with this year's team.

"This is a different team," Dungy said. "We're not playing quite as sharp as we did last year, but we're finding ways to win. We're in a lot more close games, and it just seems like every week it's someone else, some other unit and whatever it takes that particularly week.

"That's good. I like that about our guys." **XLI**

Sunday, November 12, 2006

TOUGH ROAD TO HISTORY

Colts Beat Buffalo Bills, 17-16, to Improve to 9-0

Maybe history isn't supposed to come easy.

It certainly didn't for the Colts Sunday.

Because of that, much of the talk in the Colts post-game locker room following a 17-16 victory over the Buffalo Bills in front of 57,306 at the RCA Dome Sunday afternoon was about what Indianapolis didn't do.

The Colts didn't protect the ball as they usually do.

They didn't score as they usually do.

And they certainly didn't make things as comfortable for the home fans as they often do.

But here's what the Colts did do:

They pushed closer to a fourth consecutive AFC South title.

They won for the 31st time in the last 34 regular-season games, and also won for the 30th consecutive regular-season game in which they had not yet clinched their playoff seeding.

They became the first team in NFL history to start back-to-back seasons 9-0.

Mostly, Colts quarterback Peyton Manning said, they won.

Which he said is really all that mattered.

"You harp on the win – it was a good win," said Manning, who completed 27 of 39 passes for 236 yards and a touchdown and did thrown an interception for the sixth time in nine games this season.

"You never take a win for granted," added Manning, who gave the Colts a 7-3 lead with a 1-yard touchdown pass to wide receiver Reggie Wayne with 11:09 remaining in the second quarter, after which they never trailed. "I learned that at an early age. When you go 3-13 your rookie year, you learn that fast. The idea is to keep winning and keep improving at the same time."

So, it was by one point over a team with three victories . . .

So, the Colts committed two turnovers and forced none . . .

So, Bills kicker Rian Lindell missed 41-yard field goal with less than seven minutes remaining and Buffalo trailing, 17-16.

So what?, Colts players said.

"Call it ugly – whatever you want to call it," Colts

Buffalo Bills at Indianapolis Colts

Score by Quarters	1	2	3	4	Score
Buffalo Bills	3	7	3	3	16
Indianapolis Colts	0	10	7	0	17

Going 9-0 for the second season in a row was tougher than they thought, but the Colts defense helped scratch out a 17-16 victory against the Bills.

rookie running back Joseph Addai said. "We got a W out of it. That was the biggest thing."

The Colts, after taking a 17-10 early in the second half on a 5-yard run by Joseph Addai, did not score again, punting twice in the third quarter and losing possession when veteran running back Dominic Rhodes fumbled at the Colts 45 after a 4-yard gain with just under nine minutes remaining.

Lindell's missed 41-yarder came on the ensuing possession, after which the Colts drained the final 6:22 from the clock with a 10-play game-clinching drive.

The Colts, maligned throughout the season defensively, held the Bills to 162 total yards, 101 after the first possession. That was the lowest yardage total for a Colts opponent this season. They also registered four sacks, matching their season-high.

The Colts (9-0), the NFL's last remaining unbeaten team, increased their lead in the AFC South to four games over Jacksonville (5-4). The Jaguars lost at home, 13-10, to the Houston Texans.

The victory made the Colts the first team in NFL his-

Nick Harper helped a Colts passing defense that allowed just 51 net passing yards against Buffalo.

tory to start back-to-back seasons with nine consecutive victories. The Colts and the 1929-31 Green Bay Packers had been the only teams to start consecutive seasons 8-0.

"Any time you can make history in this league, it's so special, so we're thrilled to have done that," Colts tight end Ben Utecht said.

"Hopefully, it will be 10-0 two years in a row," Colts linebacker Cato June said.

"It's great, it's history and it's very cool but it's not the focus of our season," Colts offensive tackle Ryan Diem said. "The focus of our season is to finish out the year the right way and continue winning. The records and history – that's stuff we'll dwell on later in life.

"Right now, we're focused on winning our division, going to the playoffs and finishing the job the right way."

The Colts started last season 13-0.

"Realistically, you never think you're going to run off eight, nine wins in a row in this league," Colts Head Coach

Tony Dungy said. "To do it two years in a row, is a testament to our assistant coaches, No. 1 – the way they prepare our team – and to our veteran leaders, No. 2."

Said Manning, "There are true professionals on this team, guys who take their jobs and their crafts very seriously and guys who prepare hard every single week. It's a credit to these guys, and obviously the idea is just to keep it going."

Asked to compare this year's team to last year, Dungy said, "I think we're just as talented. I think our offense in a lot of ways is playing better. We miss (wide receiver) Brandon Stokley (out seven of nine games with injuries) and I think our offensive game can still ratchet it up some when he gets back. Defensively, we're not playing as sharp. . . .

"We had the same record, but we are not playing as well as last year."

The Colts, who will visit Dallas (4-4 entering Sunday's game) next week, snapped a 10-10 halftime tie when rookie running back Joseph Addai scored on a 5-yard run to cap a nine-play, 74-yard drive. That made it, 17-10, Colts.

That was the Colts second seven-point lead of the game. They had led 10-3 in the second quarter before a 68-yard fumble return by cornerback Terrence McGee with 31 seconds remaining in the second quarter. On the play, Manning completed a short pass to tight end Ben Utecht, who fumbled near the Bills 32.

"At least a 10-point swing – probably a 14-point swing," Manning said.

The Colts had scored on their previous two possessions and had driven from their 9 to the Bills 43 before the fumble.

"We were kind of in a rhythm and had them on their heels a little bit," Manning said. "It was a great play by them."

McGee wasn't finished with the fumble return.

On the play after Addai's touchdown, McGee returned a kickoff 88 yards to the Colts 12. Bills kicker Rian Lindell's 30-yard field goal four plays later cut the Colts lead to 17-13.

With the Bills leading, 3-0, after the first quarter, the Colts took a 10-3 lead on a 1-yard touchdown pass from Manning to Wayne and a 41-yard field goal by kicker Adam Vinatieri.

Vinatieri's field goal came with 2:44 remaining, and when the Colts stopped the Bills' ensuing drive, the Colts had a chance to take a two-score lead before McGee's fumble return.

The Colts never trailed after Wayne's second-quarter touchdown, but they were tied, and didn't clinch the victory until the game's final drive.

After Lindell missed from 41 yards, 6:22 remained. Addai rushed six times for 37 yards, the Colts produced four first downs and Buffalo never took possession again.

"There are no easy games in this league and every week is tough," Dungy said. "We found that out today. If you're not on your game, it doesn't matter who you play, where you play, you're going to have trouble. . . .

"Games are tough. We got our ninth win. We know we're going to have to play better next week, so we'll go to work on that."

And Dungy said the Colts will do that work knowing they can still improve, and knowing they must improve in the final seven games of the season.

"We haven't had a 60-minute game," Dungy said. "We haven't had a game where all three units came out and got the job done. . . .

"We've got a lot better football we can play in the second half of the year."

Said June, "We can't sit back on anything right now. We're looking to move forward and keep improving. We're looking to be the first team to be 10-0 two years in a row." **XLI**

Sunday, November 19, 2006

BURNED IN BIG D

Colts Lose to Dallas, 21-14, in Texas Stadium

Tony Dungy saw it very simply.

Too many mistakes.

Too many turnovers.

Too many lost opportunities.

"When you play a good team, mistakes are going to cost you," the Colts Head Coach said.

And on Sunday, they cost the Colts big-time.

The Colts, who entered the weekend as the NFL's last remaining unbeaten team, became the last team in the league to lose in the 2006 regular season Sunday, losing to the Dallas Cowboys, 21-14, in front of 63,706 at Texas Stadium.

"Everybody knows it's not the end of the world, but at this point, no one likes to lose, especially when you didn't play your best and didn't go out there and get the job done," Colts linebacker Cato June said.

The Colts (9-1), who lost for just the fourth time in their last 35 regular-season games, committed four turnovers, two lost fumbles and two interceptions, one of which was an interception returned for a 39-yard touchdown early in the second half.

They also dropped at least one interception, and late in the game, had an interception reversed because of a defensive holding penalty.

They were uncharacteristic errors, Dungy said, but they were the kinds of mistakes the Colts have made a bit more in recent weeks.

In the past few games, the Colts overcame those errors. On Sunday, they couldn't."

"We've had some of this show up in the past," Dungy said. "We've been able to dodge bullets. Today, we couldn't dodge a bullet."

The Colts, with their nine consecutive victories to start the season, became the first team in NFL history to start consecutive seasons with 9-0 records.

"We have to go back and get another streak started," Dungy said.

"I don't think this game had much to do with the other games," said Colts quarterback Peyton Manning, who completed 20 of 39 passes for 254 yards and two touchdowns with two interceptions for a season-low passer rating of 67.7.

Indianapolis Colts at Dallas Cowboys

Score by Quarters	1	2	3	4	Score
Indianapolis Colts	0	7	7	0	14
Dallas Cowboys	0	0	7	14	21

While the loss to Dallas may have dimmed the spotlight on an undefeated season,
the Colts maintained tunnel vision in their march to the playoffs.

"This was about Dallas out-executing us. They made more plays than we did. We got some turnovers defensively, but it was kind of off-set by the turnovers we had offensively. You can't turn it over that many times on the road against a good team like Dallas.

"You've just to give them credit. They just outplayed us."

Particularly in the second half, a half that began with a 39-yard interception return for a touchdown by Cowboys linebacker Kevin Burnett and a half in which Dallas outscored the Colts, 21-7.

After holding the Cowboys scoreless in the first half, a half in which they allowed just 134 total yards and seven first downs, the Colts defense allowed 14 second-half

The Colts could not extend their winning streak in Dallas, suffering their first loss of the season.

points and 208 total yards.

The Cowboys outscored the Colts 14-0 in the fourth quarter, with running back Marion Barber capping two long touchdown drives with runs of 5 yards and 1 yard.

His five-yarder with 11:36 remaining tied it 14-14.

His 1-yarder with 6:00 remaining was the game-winner.

"There were some plays to be made and we didn't make them," Colts defensive tackle Anthony "Booger" McFarland said. "In this type of game, if you don't make those plays, you're not going to win.

Colts vs Cowboys

"I don't care who you are. You can't win with mistakes – offense, defense, special teams. You just can't win. You have to be able to limit your mistakes. I don't care if you're 9-0 or 0-9. You have to not make mistakes, and you have to be able to make the swing plays in the fourth quarter.

"Today, you have to take your hats off to the Cowboys. They made them and we didn't."

The Colts now lead the AFC South by three and a half games over Jacksonville. The Jaguars play host to the New York Giants Monday night.

"Fundamental football still wins in this league," Dungy said. "You can't do the things we did today and win. We've had some of this show up in the past and we've been able to overcome it, but you're playing with fire.

"Today, the fire caught us."

For the Colts, the turnovers started early. They fumbled three times in the first quarter, losing two. The Cowboys recovered fumbles by Manning and wide receiver Marvin Harrison as the Colts managed 42 yards offense in the quarter.

The Cowboys couldn't take advantage because Indianapolis forced Dallas into mistakes, too. On the Cowboys' first series, Indianapolis defensive end Dwight Freeney sacked Cowboys quarterback Tony Romo, forcing a fumble that linebacker Cato June recovered.

Later in the quarter, Colts cornerback Nick Harper intercepted a deep pass from Romo at the Cowboys 9.

The Colts got a late touchdown pass from Manning to wide receiver Reggie Wayne just before the end of the second quarter and entered halftime with a 7-0 lead.

"We felt pretty good," Dungy said. "We had a seven-point lead and we were getting the ball to start the second half. We felt like if we could get up two scores, we could put some pressure on them and force them into a throwing game."

Instead, the Cowboys tied the game, 7-7, when linebacker Kevin Burnett returned an interception 39 yards for a touchdown on the Colts first possession of the second half.

"It was that type of game," Dungy said.

The Colts failed to score on their next drive, but late in the third quarter, they drove for a touchdown that gave them a one-touchdown lead.

After a Dallas punt, the Colts drove 80 yards on 10 plays, with Colts quarterback Peyton Manning throwing four yards to tight end Dallas Clark for a touchdown and a 14-7 Indianapolis lead.

The Cowboys tied the game with a 68-yard, 15-play drive that ended with Barber's 5-yard run. After the Colts failed to pick up a first down on the ensuing drive, Dallas used seven plays to drive 80 yards, taking its first lead on Barber's one-yard run.

The Colts, who rallied for come-from-behind fourth-quarter victories against Tennessee, Denver and the New York Jets this season, drove 62 yards to the Dallas 8, but on 4th-and-2 – after an incomplete pass to tight end Ben Utecht on third down – Manning's pass to the back of the end zone was also incomplete.

"We've been in similar situations in the past where we had made plays," Manning said. "Today, we didn't."

Said Clark, "You just can't make those mistakes and you've just got to execute better against opponents like that. They made the plays they had to."

"It's always disappointing when you don't win, and this was a very disappointing game," Dungy said. "I thought Dallas played very well. They came out with a lot of energy. They were very physical and they came out hitting. It was that type of game, where you were going to have to play fundamental football. We weren't able to do that today. . . .

"They made the plays and we couldn't today." XLI

Sunday, November 26, 2006

PASSION AND ENERGY

Colts Run Past Eagles, 45-21, in Prime-Time Game in RCA Dome

A week after their first loss of the season, the Colts talked this past week about playing with passion and energy when they returned home on Sunday night in front of a national television audience.

The Colts rocked, and they rolled. But mostly, they ran. And they ran.

And they ran.

Given a chance to extend their AFC South lead, and given a chance to impress a national-television audience, the Colts did just that, and did so with their most impressive running performance of the season. Rookie running back Joseph Addai rushed for a season-high 171 yards and four touchdowns and the Colts beat the Philadelphia Eagles, 45-21, in front of 57,296 at the RCA Dome Sunday night.

"We talked about – last night and today – playing with passion, playing with energy," Colts Head Coach Tony Dungy said. "I thought we did that. We came out and we played very hard. We made some things happen.

"I thought we came out early, kept the crowd in it, and I thought it was probably the best we played at home all year."

The Colts, who have won 17 of their past 18 regular-season home games, finished with a season-high 237 yards rushing, including 68 from starter Dominic Rhodes.

"I thought Joe and Dom both ran well," said Colts quarterback Peyton Manning, who completed 14 of 20 passes for 183 yards and a touchdown with an interception for a passer rating of 94.4. "We've had a good system all season, and it was good run-blocking tonight by the offensive line and the tight ends.

"Those guys (Addai and Rhodes) did a good job making guys miss on their own."

Addai's four touchdowns rushing tied the Colts record set by Eric Dickerson in a Monday Night victory over Denver in 1988.

Addai scored on touchdown runs of 15, 10 and 15 yards in the first half as the Colts – who lost to Dallas, 21-14, a week ago – took a 24-7 halftime lead. The first-half performance tied the Colts franchise record for touchdowns by a rookie in a game.

Philadelphia Eagles at Indianapolis Colts

Score by Quarters	1	2	3	4	Score
Philadelphia Eagles	0	7	7	7	21
Indianapolis Colts	7	17	7	14	45

Joseph Addai had the best game of his promising young career with 171 yards on 24 carries and four TDs.

The Eagles, after trailing 31-7 early in the third quarter, pulled to within 10 points – 31-21 – early in the fourth, but could get no closer.

The victory moved the Colts (10-1), the three-time defending AFC South champions, a game closer to a fourth consecutive division title. The Colts lead the South by four games over the Jacksonville Jaguars (6-5), 27-24 losers to the Buffalo Bills Sunday.

The Colts can clinch the division with a victory at Tennessee Sunday.

"We had a good week of practice," Manning said. "Guys were disappointed after last week's game, and they wanted to get a win and try to get that taste out of your mouth."

The victory also enabled the Colts – who lost for the first time this season a week ago, 21-14 to Dallas – to maintain a one-game lead in the race for home-field advantage in the AFC playoffs. The Baltimore Ravens and San Diego Chargers have 9-2 records, and are a game behind Indianapolis.

"You know how our veteran guys are going to go in practice," Dungy said. "They went that way, so you felt like they were going to come out and play well. It was a disappointed team on the plane ride home and I just hoped we'd come out and play not too overanxious. I felt we did."

Said Colts defensive tackle Raheem Brock, "Coming off that loss, we wanted to get back on track – especially our defense. I think we did that tonight."

The Colts, who led the AFC South by three games entering the weekend, took the opening kickoff and drove 79 yards on nine plays, taking the lead when Addai capped the drive with a 15-yard run.

Kicker Adam Vinatieri's point-after made it 7-0, Colts,

Reggie Wayne made a circus catch among his four grabs for 77 yards and a touchdown.

with 10:06 remaining in the first quarter. The Eagles drove deep into Colts territory on their first possession, but the drive stalled at the Colts 18.

Eagles kicker David Akers, normally one of the NFL's most reliable kickers, missed a 36-yard field goal and the Colts maintained their lead. When the quarter ended, the Colts had driven to the Eagles 10, largely because of the running of Addai and a spectacular, one-handed, 38-yard reception by wide receiver Reggie Wayne.

Addai rushed for two more touchdowns in the second quarter – a 10-yarder with 14:55 remaining before halftime and another 15-yarder with 8:58

Ryan Diem and the line led an efficient offense that gained 420 net yards against Philadelphia and scored the game's first 21 points.

tory, and kicker Adam Vinatieri's 44-yard field goal on the last play of the half gave Indianapolis a 24-7 lead.

Early in the third quarter, the Colts extended the lead, driving 89 yards on nine plays, a drive capped by Manning's first touchdown pass of the game and 21st of the season – an 11-yard strike to Wayne in the back of the end zone.

The Eagles, losers of five of their last six games, reduced the lead to 17 points when quarterback Jeff Garcia passed three yards to wide receiver Reggie Brown for a touchdown late in the third quarter.

They then trimmed the lead to 10, 31-21, with a 6-yard run by Brian Westbrook, with 10:13 remaining, but the Colts drove the length of the field, extending the lead to 38-21, on Addai's fourth touchdown with 3:38 remaining.

The Colts then further secured the victory when cornerback Kelvin Hayden returned a fumble 26 yards for a touchdown with 3:25 remaining. Defensive end Robert Mathis sacked Eagles quarterback Jeff Garcia, forcing the fumble.

"It was a good win for us, and really nice to bounce back and play well after we didn't play well last week," Dungy said.

remaining in the second quarter.

The Eagles pulled to within two touchdowns, 21-7, with 1:19 remaining in the second quarter when quarterback Jeff Garcia passed one yard to tight end L.J. Smith. Manning then drove the Colts into Eagles terri-

"This got us back to our swagger, to playing with excitement and with passion," Colts offensive tackle Tarik Glenn said. "That's what Coach Dungy talked about all week. We felt like we had to come out and play Colts football for 60 minutes.

"Pretty much, except for a couple of glitches, that's what we did." **XLI**

Sunday, December 3, 2006

A PAINFUL LOSS

Sixty-Yard Field Goal Beats Colts, 20-17, in Tennessee

The Colts traveled South looking to make history.

They made it. Just not the kind they wanted.

With a chance to clinch a franchise-record fourth consecutive AFC South title with a victory, the Colts instead squandered a 14-point lead for the first time in Colts Head Coach Tony Dungy's tenure with the team.

That helped prevent any celebrating by the Colts Sunday afternoon.

The legs of Vince Young hurt, too.

A miracle field goal hurt a lot more.

Rob Bironas, a second-year kicker for the Tennessee Titans, kicked the fourth-longest field goal in NFL history – a 60-yarder with seven seconds remaining – lifting the resurgent Titans (5-7) to a 20-17 come-from-behind victory over the Colts (10-2) in front of 69,143 at LP Field Sunday afternoon.

"It's the first time we've lost a two-touchdown lead since I've been here and it doesn't feel very good," said Dungy, who never had lost a game as head coach in which his team held a lead of 14 points or more. "I thought Tennessee played very well and they took the game from us. . . .

"They make a 60-yard field goal – you take your hat off to them. You put yourself in that position, where a field goal beats you . . . it did."

The loss, the Colts second in as many road games, kept the Colts from clinching a fourth consecutive AFC South title.

"Losing is no fun – it's awful," said Colts quarterback Peyton Manning, who completed 21 of 28 passes for 351 yards and a touchdown with two interceptions for a passer rating of 98.8.

"It's miserable. It rips your guts out. We don't like to do it. This one hurts. We have to let it sting tonight and regroup. We've got a tough one down in Jacksonville next week."

Said Colts defensive tackle Raheem Brock, "It's a tough loss. They outplayed us. You've got to give hats off to them."

The second-place Jacksonville Jaguars (6-5) played the Miami Dolphins in Miami at 4 p.m. Sunday. The Colts could still clinch the division with a Jaguars loss.

Indianapolis Colts at Tennessee Titans

Score by Quarters	1	2	3	4	Score
Indianapolis Colts	7	7	0	3	17
Tennessee Titans	0	10	0	10	20

Despite the appearance of their playmaking safety Bob Sanders, who played in only four regular season games due to injuries, the Colts could not beat the Titans.

The Colts visit the Jaguars Sunday at 1 p.m.

"We had a chance to get something done today and we didn't do it," Dungy said. "We've got to bounce back. We're going to have the same situation next week – a very hostile environment, a tough team that plays us well. We've got to go win a game next week."

The loss snapped the Colts 12-game winning streak against AFC South teams. In the first half of the season, the Colts swept Tennessee, Houston and Jacksonville at the RCA Dome.

"It's disappointing – no question about it," Manning said. "It's always tough to beat a division team a second time when you play at their place. We knew it was going to be a tough game coming on. We had opportunities and just didn't get it done."

The Titans, after falling behind 14-0 late in the first half, rallied with 10 points in the final two minutes of the second quarter, then took the lead when Young – their starting quarterback and the No. 3 overall selection in last April's NFL Draft – threw a 9-yard touchdown pass to wide receiver Brandon Jones with 12:24 remaining.

Colts kicker Adam Vinatieri's 20-yard field goal with 2:38 remaining tied it at 17-17, but Young rallied the Texans for a second consecutive week.

Young, who last week rallied the Titans from a 21-0 fourth-quarter deficit for a 24-21 victory over the New York Giants, drove the Titans to the Colts 42.

There, facing 4th-and-11, Titans Head Coach Jeff Fisher first sent the field-goal unit onto the field. He then changed his mind and sent the punt team on, but after called a timeout, Fisher sent the field goal team back on.

Bironas' 60-yarder sailed through the uprights, setting off a raucous celebration.

"It's disappointing," Colts wide receiver Brandon Stokley said. "We just didn't make enough plays. We had opportunities and they made more plays than we did. That's the bottom line in this game. We didn't make the

Offensive guard Jake Scott has been a mainstay on the offensive line since starting as a rookie midway through the 2004 season.

plays at the end."

Said Manning, "Obviously, you'd rather have the ball last. That's always been my philosophy – that I'd rather have the ball in our hands with a chance. There certainly was a lot of wind out there – no question that was a real factor, them having the wind with them in the fourth quarter for that field-goal attempt. That was a heck of a kick. . . .

"They made more plays than we did. That's usually what it comes down to – the team that makes the most plays on that day is usually going to win."

The Colts, after dominating the first half statistically, maintained a four-point lead throughout the third quarter, holding the Titans scoreless in the period but also failing to score. The Colts finished the period leading the Titans, 14-10.

"They've been a fourth quarter team," Colts middle

Bryan Fletcher caught three passes for 56 yards against Tennessee.

The Manning-to-Harrison touchdown came on 3rd-and-10 from the Colts 32 and gave the Colts an early lead with 3:51 remaining in the first quarter. It was the 100th time in their nine seasons together the two had combined for a touchdown.

That extended the NFL record the two already hold for touchdowns by a quarterback-receiver tandem. Steve Young and Jerry Rice of the San Francisco 49ers previously held the record and are in second place with 85.

Earlier in the quarter, Titans linebacker Peter Sirmon intercepted a pass from Manning that caromed off Harrison. Two plays later, Colts cornerback Jason David intercepted Young, setting up Manning's touchdown to Harrison.

The Colts extended the lead to two touchdowns on their ensuing possession, driving 81 yards on 14 plays and using 8:01.

Starting running back Dominic Rhodes capped the drive with a 2-yard run with 7:18 remaining, giving the Colts a 14-0 lead.

The Titans cut the lead to 14-3 with 1:49 remaining in the half when Rob Bironas converted a 25-yard field goal, then a Colts turnover changed the game's momentum.

With just under a minute remaining in the half, Manning threw to Colts tight end Bryan Fletcher, but Titans linebacker Keith Bulluck made a diving interception at the Colts 42.

"They got back in it," Stokley said. "They played hard. They didn't give up. They made some plays when it counted. They seemed to make a few more than we did and that's why they won."

Three plays later, Young threw a 20-yard touchdown pass to wide receiver Drew Bennett to cut the Colts lead to 14-10 and set the tone for a dramatic second half. Colts kicker Adam Vinatieri then missed a 53-yard field goal on the last play of the half. **XLI**

linebacker Gary Brackett said. "They're great in the second half. It was up to us to get it out of reach and we weren't able to do it."

The Titans had a chance to take a lead on their first possession of the quarter, but Colts cornerback/safety Marlin Jackson intercepted Titans quarterback Vince Young in the end zone to end the drive.

The Colts then drove to the Titans 46, but after wide receiver Brandon Stokley couldn't hold a pass from quarterback Peyton Manning, the Titans forced a punt.

The Colts, who had 278 yards offense in the first two quarters, spent the first 28 minutes of the first half building a lead. The Titans spent the final two minutes cutting into it.

The Colts, after an early exchange of interceptions, took a 7-0 lead with a 68-yard touchdown pass from Manning to wide receiver Marvin Harrison, who finished with seven receptions for 178 yards.

Sunday, December 10, 2006

DISAPPOINTED AGAIN

Colts Lose to Jacksonville Jaguars, 44-17, in Jacksonville

New week, same story.

Except this time, the story had a more convincing twist. The Colts, for a second consecutive week, traveled to a division opponent with a chance to clinch their fourth consecutive AFC South title. And for a second consecutive week, they traveled home disappointed, the season's primary goal unaccomplished.

A week ago, the disappointment was sudden and unexpected.

On Sunday, it was thorough.

On a cool, bright afternoon on which Jacksonville Jaguars rookie running back Maurice Jones-Drew set a franchise record for all-purpose yards, the Colts allowed the second-most rushing yards in an NFL game since 1970, losing to the Jaguars, 44-17, in front of 67,164 at Alltel Stadium.

"We didn't play as well as we can play," Colts Head Coach Tony Dungy said. "We can play a lot better than that. We're going to have to.

"Our trick, our task, is to get back going and play better. I believe we will."

The Colts (10-3), who entered the weekend with a three-game lead in the AFC South, still lead the division by two games over Jacksonville (8-5).

After winning their first nine games of the season, the Colts have lost three of their last four games and for the third time in as many road games.

"When you lose, it rips you apart," Colts quarterback Peyton Manning said.

"Fortunately for us, we're 10-3," Colts defensive tackle Anthony "Booger" McFarland said. "At the end of the day, we're still somewhere near the top of the AFC. It could be the No. 1 spot. It's a good position to have problems.

"Now, you've got to do something. Otherwise, you're just going to waste a lot of hard work and a lot of effort."

Said Colts running back Joseph Addai, "I don't think we should be getting down right now. Right now, we should be lifting each other up and getting ready for next week."

The first two losses of the season were decided in the fourth quarter, with the Dallas Cowboys rallying from a seven-point fourth-quarter deficit for a 21-14 victory

Indianapolis Colts at Jacksonville Jaguars

Score by Quarters	1	2	3	4	Score
Indianapolis Colts	3	7	0	7	17
Jacksonville Jaguars	7	17	13	7	44

Although Reggie Wayne had eight catches for 110 yards, the rest of the Colts team had a tough day against the Jaguars.

and the Tennessee Titans converting a 60-yard field goal in the final 10 seconds last week for a 20-17 victory.

Sunday's game wasn't nearly as close.

The Jaguars, who entered the game as the NFL's third-ranked rushing offense, finished the game with 375 yards rushing on 42 attempts, the most yards rushing ever allowed by Indianapolis in a single game.

"Those guys ran through us," Dungy said.

Asked if the team's confidence had been damaged, Dungy said, "I'm sure it is after a couple of games like we've had – the second half last week and this game this week – but we've got to bounce back. The thing we have to do is nothing spectacular. It's not changing anything. It's doing what we're capable of doing and doing it more often. We'll get that done. We've got a lot of veteran guys who have been here before."

Jones-Drew, a second-round selection in this past April's NFL Draft from UCLA, rushed for 166 yards and two touchdowns on 15 carries, while veteran running back Fred Taylor added 131 yards and a touchdown on nine carries.

Jones-Drew, who also returned a kickoff for a touchdown, finished with a franchise-record 303 all-purpose yards.

The Jaguars averaged 8.6 yards per rush.

The Colts, after taking a 10-7 lead midway through the second quarter, allowed 30 consecutive points, as the sold-out crowd at Alltel Stadium celebrated.

"It's one of those things where everything went haywire," Dungy said.

After taking their only lead with 8:18 remaining before halftime, the Colts went five consecutive series without scoring, managing just four first downs during

Hunter Smith ranked third in the AFC with a 44.4-yard punting average.

that decisive stretch.

"We need to play better offensively," said Manning, who completed 25 of 50 passes for 313 yards and no touchdowns with one interception for a passer rating of 61.5. "We need to stay on the field, make more plays and score more points, is what it comes down to. . . .

"We need to improve. We need to get better. It's not enough to say, 'Things are going to get fixed. Things are going to get better.' You've got to go out and do it. That starts on the practice field."

Colts vs Jaguars

The Jaguars, who entered the weekend trailing the Colts by three games in the AFC South, turned in a dominant first quarter, and except for a brief second-quarter Indianapolis rally, controlled much of the game.

The Jaguars took an early lead with a two-play, 94-yard drive that Jones-Drew capped with an 18-yard run with 12:19 remaining. Taylor had the key play on the drive, running through the middle for a 76-yard gain to the Colts 18.

On the previous possession, the Colts drove to the Jaguars 44, where the drive stalled after Colts wide receiver Brandon Stokley dropped a pass in the end zone from Manning.

Colts kicker Adam Vinatieri made it 7-3, Jaguars, with 6:05 remaining in the quarter when he converted a 41-yard field goal.

The Jaguars had the ball inside Colts territory three times in the quarter, but managed to score just once. Kicker Josh Scobee missed a 48-yard field goal with 3:53 remaining in the quarter, during which the Jaguars out-gained the Colts, 133-65.

The Jaguars, who finished the first half with 251 yards and three touchdowns rushing, pulled away in the second quarter with 21-yard touchdown run by Taylor and a 48-yarder by Jones-Drew.

On the drive just before Taylor's touchdown, Colts running back Dominic Rhodes' 1-yard run with 8:18 remaining before halftime gave Indianapolis a 10-7 lead. The Colts didn't score again until 11:13 remaining in the game. The Jaguars led by then, 37-10.

Jones-Drew returned the opening kickoff of the second half 93 yards for a touchdown to put the Jaguars ahead, 31-10, and Scobee all but ended any hopes of an Indianapolis rally with third-quarter field goals of 34 and 46 yards.

A 1-yard sneak by Manning made it 37-17, Jaguars,

early in the fourth quarter, but Jaguars running back Alvin Pearman's six-yard run with 3:59 pushed the Jaguars' lead back to the final margin of 27, the Colts widest margin of defeat in Dungy's five-season tenure.

Afterward, Dungy said the season was far from over, and pointed to the 1999 season as proof. In that season, Dungy was the head coach of the Tampa Bay Buccaneers when they were shutout, 45-0, late in the season by the Oakland Raiders before rallying to make the NFC Championship Game.

"I've been in ones tougher than this," Dungy said. "We have to bounce back. I think we have the people in there who can do that. I've been in this situation before, and actually had a game much worse than this when I was in a playoff run in Tampa.

"We lost a game, 45-0, that wasn't even this good and came back and went to the championship game.

"I've got a lot of faith in our guys and I think we'll bounce back."

Said Colts middle linebacker and defensive captain Gary Brackett, "After losing the way we did today, some teams fall apart. I guess you really see a team's desire after you lose like this. I'm betting on us to step back up and put the pieces back together."

Brackett spoke in a quiet, subdued Colts locker room, and on the other side of the room, Manning – the Colts two-time Most Valuable Player and offensive captain – echoed Brackett's sentiments.

"Talk is one thing," Manning said. "We're kind of in a Show-Me mode as opposed to talking about it. You're not going to get a lot of words from me today. It's about going to work and correcting mistakes and trying to improve as a football player, which hopefully should improve your football team.

"Talk doesn't carry a lot of weight right now, except what the head coach says...." **XLI**

Monday, December 18, 2006

PRIME-TIME PERFORMANCE

Colts Pull Away from Cincinnati for 34-16 Victory on
Monday Night Football

The Colts heard the talk – all of it.

How they were struggling on defense.

How they had too many injuries.

Mainly this past week Colts players heard how after three losses in four games they were too inconsistent on offense, couldn't stop the run on defense and could not overcome personnel losses all around the roster.

The Colts heard . . .

But they didn't listen.

Peyton Manning threw a season-high four touchdown passes, and the Colts defense – maligned much of the past week — turned in one of its best performances of the season against one of the NFL's top offenses as the Colts beat the Cincinnati Bengals, 34-16, in front of 57,292 fans at the RCA Dome.

"Obviously, very proud of our team tonight," Colts Head Coach Tony Dungy said. "We played hard and we played with a passion."

The victory snapped the Colts first two-game regular-season winning streak of the season, and the first two-game losing streak in games with playoff implications since the middle of the 2004 season.

The Bengals (8-6) entered the game with a four-game winning streak, having allowed 17 points in the last three games.

"It was just a good team win," said Manning, the Colts six-time Pro Bowl quarterback who completed 29 of 36 passes for 282 yards and four touchdowns with no interceptions for a passer rating of 136.3.

"Two losses is kind of unfamiliar territory. A gal at ESPN asked me what it felt like to be scoring all those points, like it was a new feeling. The past two weeks have been kind of unfamiliar. Not something we wanted to continue.

"We wanted to answer the bell, answer the challenge."

Manning, the 2003 and 2004 National Football League Most Valuable Player, threw touchdowns of 4, 1 and 3 yards to seven-time Pro Bowl wide receiver Marvin Harrison.

Manning also threw an 18-yard third-quarter touch-

Cincinnati Bengals at Indianapolis Colts

Score by Quarters	1	2	3	4	Score
Cincinnati Bengals	3	7	3	3	16
Indianapolis Colts	3	14	14	3	34

Dwight Freeney posted a seasonal-best three sacks in the Colts 34-16 victory against Cincinnati.

down pass to wide receiver Reggie Wayne.

"It's like when you have Michael Jordan," Dungy said of Manning, a two-time NFL Most Valuable Player. "You feel like you're in every game."

The Colts did not punt until the fourth quarter, and the only possessions before that that did not end in a score came when punt returner Terrence Wilkins muffed a first-half punt and when the Colts were stopped on downs early in the second half.

"Today we knew we had to go out and prove a point, that we ain't pretenders – we're contenders," Colts running back Dominic Rhodes said. "Everybody was talking about what we can't do, what we ain't going to do. We showed what we are going to do and how we're going to do it.

"That was Colts football we played."

The victory came a day after the Colts (11-3) clinched a fourth consecutive AFC South title with the Tennessee Titans' 24-17 victory over Jacksonville.

It also enabled the Colts – who are now 7-0 in the RCA Dome this season – to maintain their hold the No. 2 seed in the AFC. They remain one game behind AFC-leading San Diego and hold the second position over the Baltimore Ravens (10-3) because of a better strength-of-victory rating.

The top two seeds in each conference earn first-round postseason bye and a home playoff game in the Divisional Playoff round January 13-14.

"The thing I was proud about our guys is we didn't look at it like it was a crisis," Dungy said. "I know everybody talked about that, but you'd seen it all through the league – teams not playing their best for a week or two. We knew we were still in good position.

"What we've got to do now is see if we can build on this. We've got to come back and play another good game this week. We've been playing well at home and winning at home. Now, we've got to take that on the road this week. . . .

Tight End Ben Utecht became a key component of the Colts passing attack in 2006. He finished fourth on the club with 37 receptions.

"That was a good football team we beat. They were playing hot. On tape the last four weeks, they were playing as well as anyone I'd seen."

The Colts defense, which entered the game last in the NFL against the run, allowed just 278 yards – 133 rushing – and one touchdown to the NFL's seventh-ranked offense.

The touchdown came on a 25-yard drive following a Colts turnover.

A week after allowing 375 yards rushing to the Jacksonville Jaguars, it was the Colts defense that made a big play to give Indianapolis early momentum.

Defensive end Dwight Freeney, a Pro Bowl selection the past three seasons, broke free around left tackle on the Bengals' first possession. Freeney, who finished with a season-high three sacks, sacked Bengals quarterback Carson Palmer, forcing a fumble that Colts defen-

Jason David and Justin Snow celebrated a key Monday Night victory over Cincinnati.

sive tackle Anthony "Booger" McFarland recovered at the Bengals 46.

Nine plays later, Colts kicker Adam Vinatieri's 30-yard field goal gave Indianapolis a 3-0 lead with 8:00 remaining in the first quarter.

"We got the lead and that was important," Dungy said.

On their next series, the Bengals drove 66 yards on 13 plays, with kicker Shayne Graham's 27-yard field goal tying it at 3-3 with 1:01 remaining in the quarter.

Manning threw a pair of short touchdown passes to Harrison – a seven-time Pro Bowl selection – in the second quarter to give the Colts a 17-10 lead at halftime.

The Colts, who had lost three of four games entering Monday night's game, took a 10-3 lead with 10:25 remaining in the second quarter when Manning threw four yards to Harrison.

The Bengals tied the game 6:49 before halftime when running back Rudi Johnson rushed 12 yards for a touchdown.

The Colts retook the lead on the next possession, driving 61 yards for a touchdown that came when Manning passed three yards to Harrison with :13 remaining in the half.

Manning completed 18 of 20 passes for 148 yards and two touchdowns in the first half, and he also led the Colts in rushing with 10 yards on two carries.

Johnson finished the first half with 64 yards on 13 carries and he rushed for 79 yards on 22 carries for the game.

Trailing by seven at halftime, the Bengals cut the lead to 17-13 with a 30-yard field goal by Graham. The Colts extended the lead to 24-13 with a one-yard pass from Manning to Harrison with 6:36 remaining in the third quarter.

The Colts extended the lead to 31-13 on their third drive of the third quarter when Manning threw an 18-yard touchdown pass to wide receiver Reggie Wayne. The Bengals never got closer than 15 points again.

"I thought our guys all week focused in on what we were trying to say and what we were trying to do," Dungy said. "We didn't do a whole lot different. We just tried to do what we're doing a little bit better. We came out and did that tonight." XLI

Sunday, December 24, 2006

TEXAS-SIZED DISAPPOINTMENT

First Loss to Houston Texans Big Blow to Colts Playoff Seeding

Tony Dungy spoke in a low, measured tone.

Moments later, Colts quarterback Peyton Manning echoed that mood, and around him, players sat for long stretches, heads down, shoulders slumped.

Dungy, in his fifth season as the Colts head coach, called what happened Sunday afternoon in Reliant Stadium one of the most disappointing moments of his tenure, and the 27-24 loss to the Houston Texans in front of an announced 70,132 received like reviews from players throughout a somber locker room.

Disappointing. Surprising.

Disheartening.

Moments after the Colts tied the game with 2:41 remaining, Texans kicker Kris Brown's 48-yard field goal sailed straight and true through the uprights with no time remaining, sending a less-than-capacity crowd into celebration and the Colts into reflective post-game.

"Just as invigorating as Monday night (a 34-16 victory over Cincinnati) was, this is disappointing for us," Dungy said moments after the Colts first loss in 10 meetings to their AFC South rival.

"It's one of the bigger disappointments we've had since I've been here. You find out about people. You find out how you bounce back from disappointment. So, we've got to come back, play well and win this coming Sunday, then come back and get ready for the playoffs. There's nothing we can do about this game right now.

"I take the blame for it, for not having us ready to go and ready to play. They outplayed us."

How disappointing was the loss?

It was particularly so for the Colts playoff positioning.

"We had our fate in our own hands and we dropped it," Colts safety Marlin Jackson said. "That's now what you want to do if you want to be a great football team."

The Colts (11-4), who last week clinched their fourth consecutive AFC South title, entered the day holding the No. 2 playoff seed in the AFC. They had been tied with the Baltimore Ravens for the position, holding the edge over Baltimore because of a better record in common games.

"The veterans certainly knew what was at stake, the guys who have been around," said Manning, who com-

Indianapolis Colts at Houston Texans

Score by Quarters	1	2	3	4	Score
Indianapolis Colts	7	7	3	7	24
Houston Texans	14	7	0	6	27

Terrence Wilkins provided a boost to the return teams in 2006. Wilkins ranked in the conference's top 10 in kickoff and punt return average.

pleted 21 of 27 passes for 205 yards and three touchdowns – two to wide receiver Marvin Harrison and one to wide receiver Aaron Moorehead.

"I'm not sure if all the young players totally understand. Maybe you have to play, and be in this league, and be in situations in playoff scenarios to understand what was at stake today. We talked about playing with a sense of urgency, playing like we were playing like we had to win to get into the playoffs – that same sense of urgency.

"That's kind of how we prepared, and I thought offensively we played kind of with that sense of urgency. We just didn't quite do it well enough."

Said Dungy, "We had a chance to come out here and keep the pressure on some other people and win a game and we didn't do that. Houston had a very good game plan, they executed it well. It was really disappointing for us not to come through with a win down here. . . .

"It looked like the game meant more to them, and that's unfortunate, because we had a lot to play for."

On Sunday, with the Colts losing, Baltimore beat the Pittsburgh Steelers to move to 12-3 on the season. The Colts now are tied with the New England Patriots – who on Sunday clinched the AFC East – for the third-best AFC record among division winners.

"This is not the time to start getting ready for a run next year," Colts middle linebacker Rob Morris said. "It's not the time to panic. It's not the time to fold. We have to go home, look in the mirror, come out next week, play with some heart, win and get some momentum.

"There's only one option, really."

Said Colts offensive tackle Tarik Glenn, "The bottom line is the game is lost. We can't go back and do anything about it. We're just going to have to play hard,

get better as a team. Whatever the scenario is when all is said and done, we're just going to have to fight our way through it."

The Colts hold the No. 3 seed over New England because of a head-to-head victory in November. Indianapolis plays host to Miami Sunday in the regular-season finale.

The No. 1 and No. 2 seeds in each conference get a first-round playoff bye and a home playoff game on January 13-14.

The No. 3 and 4 seeds play host to wild-card games on January 6-7.

The Colts, who started the season 9-0, lost for the fourth time in six games, with all four losses coming on the road. Before the streak, the Colts had won 11 of 12 road games.

"We haven't played well on the road in the last four games," Dungy said. "Every game it seems like it's gotten a little bit worse. We had the lead in the first two games (at Dallas and Houston) and lost in the fourth quarter. In this game, we never had the lead. Against Jacksonville, we had the lead early.

"We didn't play as hard and well as you need to play to win a game on the road."

The loss also was the Colts third in as many games against AFC South opponents. Before a loss to Tennessee in early December, the Colts had won 12 consecutive division games.

Sunday's loss was strikingly similar to the one in Tennessee.

In that game, the Colts tied the game, 17-17, late in the fourth quarter only to lose, 20-17, on a 60-yard field goal in the final 10 seconds.

On Sunday, the Colts never led, but tied the game with 2:41 remaining when Manning completed a seven-yard touchdown pass to Marvin Harrison.

On the ensuing kickoff, however, Texans returner Dexter Wynn returned it to the Houston 39. Three plays later, Texans quarterback David Carr threw 17 yards to Pro Bowl wide receiver Andre Johnson, and after a three-yard run by running back Ron Dayne, Carr called timeout.

After a Colts timeout, Brown's 48-yard field goal easily passed over the crossbar.

"I don't care where we play, when we play, who we play – we've got to play better than we did today," Colts defensive tackle Anthony "Booger" McFarland said.

The Texans, who entered the game 28th in the NFL in total offense and 24th in rushing at 100 yards per game, rushed for 191 yards against the Colts 32nd-ranked rushing defense. Texans running back Ron Dayne – the 1999 Heisman Trophy winner – rushed for a career-high 153 yards and two touchdowns on 32 carries.

Dayne scored on touchdown runs of 3 and 6 yards to cap the Texans' first two drives. His six-yard run on the Texans' second drive gave Houston a 14-0 lead with 5:46 remaining in the first quarter.

The Colts cut the lead on half in the ensuing series, driving 80 yards on 10 plays, a possession capped with a 37-yard touchdown pass from Manning to Harrison.

The reception was the 10th touchdown of the season for Harrison, who now has caught at least 10 touchdown passes every season since 1999.

After the Colts defense forced a Texans punt, Manning led the Colts on a second consecutive 80-yard drive, tying the score, 14-14, with an 8-yard touchdown pass to reserve wide receiver Aaron Moorehead.

Moorehead's touchdown, the first of his four-year NFL career, came with 8:16 remaining in the half. The Texans used eight minutes on their ensuing drive, retaking the lead on a 3-yard pass from Carr to fullback Vonta Leach with 16 seconds remaining before halftime.

Colts rookie running back Joseph Addai rushed for 69 yards on nine first-half carries, and finished with 100 yards on 15 carries, his second 100-yard game of the season. Addai also surpassed the 1,000-yard mark, becoming the fourth rookie in franchise history to do so.

The Texans dominated time of possession, and limited the Colts to seven total possessions, and although the Colts scored on four of them, that wasn't enough.

And as a result, instead of celebrating, the Colts headed home for Christmas disappointed for the fourth time in six games and again looking for answers they haven't yet found.

"It's really disappointing for us to not come through with a win down here, but that's the way everything's been this year," Dungy said. "We've been a little bit on the down. We've got to try to get back up next week, win the game and enter the playoffs with some momentum."

Said McFarland, "It's just execution, and evidently at 11-4, we've executed a lot more than we haven't. That's what we have to look at. We haven't executed every Sunday or Monday, but we have done it more times than not. We just have to make sure – starting next Sunday and in the playoffs – we do. We're in the dance.

"We just have to come out next week and get some confidence." **XLI**

Sunday, December 31, 2006

MEANING AND MOMENTUM

Colts Secure No. 3 Playoff Seed with 27-22 Victory over Miami in RCA Dome

From their most meaningful regular-season finale in four seasons, the Colts wanted several things:

1) A victory.

2) Momentum entering the post-season.

3) The No. 2 seed in the AFC playoffs.

The Colts (12-4) achieved the first two, which were in their control. They missed on the third, which was not and which – as the day wore on – became increasingly unlikely. Still, for Indianapolis, the first two were far more important, anyway.

Colts quarterback Peyton Manning, who finished the regular-season with three consecutive interceptionless games, threw his 30th and 31st touchdown passes of the season, and the Colts – who had lost four of six games – held on for a 27-22 victory over the Miami Dolphins in front of 57,310 in the regular-season finale at the RCA Dome Sunday.

"Today's win was awesome," Colts offensive tackle Tarik Glenn said. "Our team needed to solidify that playing here is going to be tough for anybody who comes in here in the playoffs. It's important to create some momentum going into the playoffs.

"The last couple of months have been an up-and-down roller coaster, but we felt that if we came out there and executed, we could do some things."

The Colts, who earlier this season clinched a fourth consecutive AFC South title, will play host to the Kansas City Chiefs (9-7) Saturday at 4:30 p.m. Kansas City made the playoffs late Sunday night when the San Francisco 49ers beat Denver, 26-23, in overtime.

The Colts entered Sunday with a chance at the No. 2 seed in the AFC playoffs and a first-round bye, but needed the Baltimore Ravens to lose to the Buffalo Bills.

Baltimore beat Buffalo, 19-7.

"As I told the team, 'Everything starts over in the playoffs,'" Colts Head Coach Tony Dungy said. "It doesn't matter what your record was, whether you were resting – whatever you were doing, it doesn't matter.

"It's how you play these next 60-minute increments. You've got to win one game, and do a good job, and win

Miami Dolphins at Indianapolis Colts

Score by Quarters	1	2	3	4	Score
Miami Dolphins	3	3	6	10	22
Indianapolis Colts	0	17	3	7	27

With this TD plunge against the Dolphins, Manning helped guide the club into the playoffs as a third seed.

that one before you can worry about the next one.

"It's just the playoffs are different and we've got to be ready."

As has been the case often this season – and in the last eight seasons – when the Colts needed a big play Sunday, they got it from Manning and wide receiver Marvin Harrison.

Manning, who finished the season with a career-low nine interceptions, threw a 27-yard touchdown pass to Harrison with 10:07 remaining in the game. That gave Indianapolis a 27-15 lead.

A late turnover led to a Dolphins touchdown, and Miami took possession with 1:03 remaining, but time ran out with the Dolphins at the Colts 43.

The victory secured for the Colts the No. 3 seed in the AFC playoffs for the third time in four seasons, and also ensured their fourth consecutive season with 12 or more victories. The Colts were the AFC's third seed in 2003 and 2004 and the No. 1 seed last season.

"It means we're doing something right in the regular season," Manning said.

Sunday's game was the first time since 2003 the Colts had played a regular-season finale with playoff implications. They clinched the No. 3 seed with a week remaining in 2004 and clinched the top seed with three weeks remaining last season.

Cato June had an interception to go along with 11 tackles and a sack as the Colts defense started clicking into gear in time for the playoffs.

"All in all, we had good intensity," Dungy said. "That's what we were looking for."

The Colts finished the 2006 regular-season unbeaten at home, the first time in the team's 23-year history in Indianapolis they have done so.

Colts vs Dolphins

The Colts last went unbeaten and untied at home in 1958, when they went 6-0 at home as the Baltimore Colts en route to he 1958 NFL Championship.

"We couldn't worry about everybody else," Colts defensive tackle Anthony "Booger" McFarland said. "We had to come out, this football team, and get our confidence, get our swagger, get our perfect record at home this year.

"That's what we did. All we talked about was controlling our fate and doing the things that we could do. We still haven't played that game we're looking for, and that's a good thing – that game where all three phases are together for 60 minutes.

"That's a good thing, that that's still out there. What a better time to have it than the playoffs."

The Dolphins, who entered the game on a two-game losing streak, took a 3-0 lead on the Colts with a 28-yard field goal by veteran kicker Olindo Mare in the first quarter of the regular-season finale Sunday.

Mare's field goal capped a 13-play, 53-yard drive that consumed 6:47.

On their first drive, the Colts received the opening kickoff and did not pick up a first down.

The Colts expected a close game, one in which points would be at a premium. In the second quarter, they played like it.

The Colts scored 10 points in the final 26 seconds of the first half, capping a wild second quarter in which the Colts turned a 3-0 deficit into an 11-point halftime lead by scoring in a variety of unusual ways.

First, with just under 13 minutes remaining in the period, Manning threw his 30th touchdown pass of the season – to defensive tackle Dan Klecko.

Klecko's 2-yard reception gave the Colts a 7-3 lead they wouldn't relinquish in the quarter, and after a 38-yard yard field goal by Mare with 1:31 remaining cut the Colts lead to one, the half got wilder.

On the drive after Mare's field goal, the Colts drove 80 yards on seven plays, with Manning running for an 11-yard touchdown with 19 seconds remaining. Manning was hit hard on the play by two Dolphins defenders as he crossed into the end zone.

"You could see how much the game meant to us," Dungy said. "Normally, he's going to slide at the 3-or-4 yard line. He worked to get it in."

On the ensuing series, Colts linebacker Cato June intercepted Dolphins quarterback Cleo Lemon and returned it eight yards to the Dolphins 37.

After a nine-yard run by rookie running back Joseph Addai, Colts kicker Adam Vinatieri's 46-yard field goal as time expired in the half made it 17-6, Colts.

Mare kicked field goals of 42 and 27 yards in the third quarter, and with Vinatieri kicking a 34-yarder in the period, the Colts led entering the fourth quarter, 20-12. Mare, who finished the day with five field goals, kicked a 34-yarder early in the fourth period to make 20-15.

But on the next possession, Harrison's 27-yard reception – his 12th touchdown of the season and seventh in the last four games – pushed the lead to 12 and helped the Colts rebound from a last-play loss to Houston last week that Dungy called one of the most disappointing in five seasons with the Colts.

"It was a tough week last week," Dungy said. "Bouncing back, coming back and trying to get that energy back and that enthusiasm – I thought we did that. I thought our offense, to put up those kinds of points on that defense was good. They hadn't really given up a ton of points to anybody. That was positive. . . .

"All in all, I thought it was a good way to end the regular season." **XLI**

Statistics

Team Statistics

	Colts	Opponents
TOTAL FIRST DOWNS	376	325
FIRST DOWNS (Rushing-Passing-By Penalty)	112 - 241 - 23	150 - 150 - 25
THIRD DOWN CONVERSIONS	105/187	90/191
FOURTH DOWN CONVERSIONS	0/4	11/14
TOTAL OFFENSIVE YARDS	6070	5316
OFFENSE (Plays-Average Yards)	1011 - 6.0	959 - 5.5
TOTAL RUSHING YARDS	1762	2768
RUSHING (Plays-Average Yards)	439 - 4.0	519 - 5.3
TOTAL PASSING YARDS	4308	2548
PASSING (Comp-Att-Int-Avg)	362 - 557 - 9 - 7.89	266 - 415 - 15 - 6.52
SACKED	15	25
FIELD GOALS	26/29	24/35
TOUCHDOWNS	50	41
(Rushing-Passing-Returns)	17 - 31 - 2	20 - 16 - 5
TIME OF POSSESSION	29:32	30:28

Passing Statistics

Player	Att	Comp	Yds	Comp %	Yds/Att	TD	TD %	INT	INT %	Long	Sack/Lost	Rating
Peyton Manning	557	362	4397	65.0	7.89	31	5.6	9	1.6	68t	14/86	101.0

Rushing Statistics

Player	No	Yds	Avg	Long	TD
Joseph Addai	226	1081	4.8	41	7
Dominic Rhodes	187	641	3.4	17	5
Peyton Manning	23	36	1.6	12	4
Ran Carthon	3	4	1.3	3t	1

Receiving Statistics

Player	No	Yds	Avg	Long	TD
Marvin Harrison	95	1366	14.4	68t	12
Reggie Wayne	86	1310	15.2	51t	9
Joseph Addai	40	325	8.1	21t	1
Ben Utecht	37	377	10.2	26	0
Dominic Rhodes	36	251	7.0	27	0
Dallas Clark	30	367	12.2	40	4
Bryan Fletcher	18	202	11.2	26	2
Brandon Stokley	8	85	10.6	23	1
Aaron Moorehead	8	82	10.3	36	1
Ricky Proehl	3	30	10.0	13	0
Dan Klecko	1	2	2.0	2	1

Field Goals

Player	1-29	20-29	30-39	40-49	50+
Adam Vinatieri	1/1	3/3	12/13	9/10	0/1
Martin Gramatica	0/0	1/1	0/0	0/0	0/0
Colts	1/1	4/4	12/13	9/10	0/1
Opponent	0/0	8/9	5/8	10/17	1/1

Punting

Player	No	Avg	Net	TB	Inside 20	Long	Blocked
Hunter Smith	47	44.4	34.5	5	14	61	0
Colts	48	43.4	34.5	5	14	61	0
Opponents	47	43.3	36.8	5	17	63	1

Punt Returns

	Ret	FC	Yards	Avg	Long	TD
Terrence Wilkins	21	13	193	9.2	82	1
T.J. Rushing	2	2	14	7.0	8	0
Colts	82t	15	207	9.0	82	1
Opponents	87t	9	327	13.1	87	1

Kickoff Returns

	No	Yards	Avg	Long	TD
Terrence Wilkins	52	1272	24.5	70	0
T.J. Rushing	2	67	33.5	47	0
Ran Carthon	2	21	10.5	21	0
Darrell Reid	1	3	3.0	3	0
Kelvin Hayden	1	1	1.0	1	0
DeDe Dorsey	0	4	0.0	4	0
Colts	58	1368	23.6	70	0
Opponents	78	2029	26.0	103	2

Defensive Leaders

		Defensive			Special Teams			Quarterback				Passes				
Rank	Name	Tackle	Solo	Asst.	Total	Solo	Asst	Sack	Yd	PR	Int	Yd	Def	B	FF	FR
1	C.June	162	85	77	0	0	0	1	3	2	3	14	2	0	2	1
2	G.Brackett	123	72	51	0	0	0	0	0	0	2	0	1	0	2	0
3	A.Bethea	105	64	41	1	1	0	0	0	0	1	38	2	0	0	0
4	R.Mathis	90	76	14	0	0	0	9.5	68.5	22	0	0	1	1	4	2
5	M.Jackson	76	49	27	11	9	2	0	0	2	1	24	1	0	0	0
6	R.Brock	74	59	15	0	0	0	3	13.5	9	0	0	0	1	3	3
7	N.Harper	73	59	14	0	0	0	0	0	0	3	18	11	0	0	0
8	G.Gardner	66	33	33	7	5	2	0	0	0	2	0	1	2	0	0
9	J.David	53	38	15	4	3	1	0	0	0	2	16	11	0	0	1
10	R.Morris	48	30	18	21	14	7	0	0	1	0	0	0	0	0	0
11	A.McFarland	45	40	5	0	0	0	2.5	11.5	0	0	0	0	0	0	1
12	D.Freeney	45	35	10	0	0	0	5.5	35.5	33	0	0	0	0	4	0
13	J.Thomas	35	29	6	0	0	0	1	8	9	0	0	0	0	0	1
14	K.Hayden	31	22	9	8	7	1	0	0	0	0	0	2	0	0	1
15	M.Doss	31	18	13	5	2	3	0	0	2	2	47	3	0	0	0
16	B.Sanders	30	20	10	0	0	0	0	0	0	1	0	1	0	1	0

Photo Gallery

Despite the challenges of the 2006 regular season, Manning kept the Colts heading in the right direction with his typical stellar play.

True Blue

Team President Bill Polian and Head Coach Tony Dungy have led a team that has produced a 60-20 record since 2002.

Colts Head Coach Ted Dungy relishes holding the Lamar Hunt Trophy.

Colts Owner and CEO Jim Irsay greets Quarterback Peyton Manning before Super Bowl XLI.

Colts President Bill Polian celebrates the Superbowl XLI victory.

Photo Gallery

Bob Sanders gets his hands on the Vince Lombardi Trophy following the Colts Super Bowl XLI victory.

Colts President Bill Polian, Colts Owner and CEO Jim Irsay and Head Coach Tony Dungy enjoy the Colts victory parade in downtown Indianapolis